Marine Corps Medals, Badges & Insignia of the Vietnam War

Dedicated to all U.S. Marine Corps Vietnam veterans and their families who supported them when they so unselfishly served their country in Vietnam

Ebook Edition ISBN - 978-1-884452-89-5
Softcover Edition ISBN - 978-1-884452-90-1

Copyright © 2025 by MOA Press

All rights reserved. No part of this publication may be reproduced, stored in retrieval systems or transmitted by any means, electronic, mechanical or by photocopying, recording or by any information storage and retrieval system without permission from the publisher, except for the inclusion of brief quotations in a review.

Press
Published by:

MOA Press (Medals of America Press)
325 Rocky Slope Road, Suite 104-234
Greenville, SC 29607
www.moapress.com • www.usmedals.com

MOA Press (Medals of America Press)
114 Southchase Blvd.
Fountain Inn, SC 29644
www.moapress.com • www.usmedals.com

Marine Corps Medals, Badges & Insignia of the Vietnam War

Table of Contents

Introduction	3
Marine Corps Insignia	6
Marine Corps Breast Insignia	10
Marine Corps Rank Insignia	13
Marine Corps Badges	18
Marine Corps Patches	23
Marine Corps Awards and Decorations	26
Marine Corps Ribbons and Devices	31
Marine Corps Military Medals	40
Foreign Military Medals	48
Issue of Medals Today	52
Marine Corps Vietnam Veterans' Awards Displays	55

For Marine Corps Vietnam War veterans and their families, military medals, insignia, and badges carry special personal and historical value. Many Vietnam veterans faced significant challenges and sacrifices during their service, including combat, injuries, and separation from loved ones. Their medals symbolize the recognition of these sacrifices and the valor they displayed in the face of adversity.

For those who lost friends and comrades during the war, military medals can serve as a solemn reminder of their sacrifices. Displaying these medals, honors the memory of those who did not return home and ensures that their legacy lives on. Earning military medals requires courage, dedication, and skill. For many veterans, their medals evoke a sense of pride in their accomplishments and the bonds forged with their fellow Marines during their time in uniform.

Service in the Marine Corps often becomes an integral part of a veteran's identity, shaping their values, beliefs, and sense of purpose. United States Marine Corps' military medals, insignia, and badges hold deep personal and symbolic meaning for Marine Corps Vietnam War veterans, representing their sacrifices, achievements, and connections to a larger community of United States military veterans. These military medals also preserve the memories and experiences of those who served for future generations to understand and appreciate.

The story of The United States Marine Corps during the Vietnam War through its symbols of valor, professional skill and identification.

Introduction

"Over 500,00 U.S. Marines have served in Vietnam. This book tells the story of the military awards they earned and the military insignia they wore that identifed them."

In 1957, the North Vietnamese led Vietcong began a rebellion against the South Vietnam government whom the U.S. supported with equipment and advisors. In August 1964, Congress passed the Tonkin Gulf Resolution giving the President the power to take "all necessary measures" to "prevent further (Communist) aggression." Between 1965 and 1969, US troop strength rose from 60,000 to over 543,000 in country. With the infusion of American arms, advice and training, the Army of the Republic of Vietnam (ARVN) and the Regional Forces and Popular Forces (RF/PF) steadily improved. The enthusiastic American units, however, tended to push the Army of South Vietnam (ARVN) aside to get into battle, a situation the ARVN, knowing it was a long war, was pleased to accept. In 1969 when the United States decided to start winding down their support in the war, the ARVN had not built up the requisite experience and confidence. The ARVN officers corps and commanders varied too widely in quality. Nevertheless, many of the ARVN units, ranging from the Airborne to individual Regional Forces (RF) companies, were excellent. The Republic of South Vietnam armed forces were in combat during most of the republic's life, at times with valor and success, but in the end not with victory. The United States aided by others came to the defense of the Republic of Vietnam in an intervention but in the end failed. American forces lost no battles, but the cost grew to high in blood, money and politics.

So putting aside the thousands of articles written by people who were not there, the war was fought with a clear mission of defending a free country against a communist invasion … and it was fought bravely and successfully by a force of mostly American and South Vietnamese troops until the January 1973 Paris Peace Agreements. Based on the Peace Agreement, U.S. forces withdrew from South Vietnam.

After the 1973 "Peace Agreement," the Army of South Vietnam (ARVN) and the People's Army of North Vietnam (PAVN) jostled for territory. In January 1975, North Vietnamese seized Phuoc Long province. When this did not bring about a United States reaction, the People's Army of North Vietnam went ahead with plans for a major offensive. After grinding and inconclusive combat north of Hue in early 1975, the People's Army of North Vietnam attacked Banmethuot in the Highlands in March. President Thieu decided to abandon the Highlands and also withdraw the Airborne Division from Central Vietnam for use as a reserve. While perhaps strategically sound, the moves provoked panic, and South Vietnam crumbled. A last-minute peace government of General Duong Van Minh was contemptuously swept aside by the victors and the Republic of Vietnam died twenty years after it was founded.

The American military was not defeated by North Vietnam's final 1975 blitzkrieg for the simple reason that there were no American military forces there to be defeated. They had left country years earlier. Ironically, that irrefutable historical fact does not seem to have registered on many Americans who still talk about America's military defeat in Vietnam. They are entitled to their own set of opinions but, as former Secretary of Defense James Schlesinger once observed, "they are not entitled to their own set of facts when it comes to shooting down Vietnam War myths, and facts".

So, this book is written for United States Marine Corps Vietnam veterans and their families in an effort to help them identify and display the military insignia and badges that represent their service in Vietnam. The majority of the Marine Corps veterans were volunteers and were joined by many young men who answered their countries call when drafted.

Of the 3,400,000 million Americans that served in the United States Armed Forces during the Vietnam War, close to 500,000 served in the United States Marine Corps. This book tells the story of the the skills they developed and the military insignia they served under. The book is not just for Vietnam veterans , but also for veterans' families. When all is said and done, it is more important for a Marine's family to gain an appreciation for the dedication and skill which went into earning these insignia.

It is the story of the Marine Corps during the Vietnam War through its symbols of professional skill and responsibilty. Every effort has been made to provide the criteria and background for each insignia and badge. However, when it came to the area of shoulder sleeve insignia, patches or as the Old Corps called them "" Battle Blazes," we could only focus on the most well known.

From the first day in the Marine Corps, every Marine begins to earn a specialty and rank insignia which indicates a skill and responsibility. For over 230 years the United States Marine Corps has developed its own unique uniform system. Initially, it was colors, a different color and unique insignia for each service as well as insignia on uniform to indicate the individual Marine's rank and responsibility from general to private.

World War II introduced individual shoulder sleeve insignia or patches for every major unit. World War II also saw different badges and ribbons awarded Marines to indicate special skills or combat experience.

So, the purpose of this book is to bring together the story and symbolism of the insignia, badges and military awards the Vietnam veteran may have earned. The United States Marine Corps insignia, badges, medals and ribbons that recognize and identify a Vietnam veterans' service.

The prestige and respect that United States Marine Corps combat veterans of the Vietnam War earned has become part of the Marine Corps culture and ethos.

Throughout its history, the Marine Corps has built a reputation for valor and bravery in combat. Marines take pride in the legacy of those who have gone before them, from the halls of Montezuma to the shores of Tripoli, and they aspire to uphold this tradition of excellence on the battlefield.

Marines undergo some of the most demanding and rigorous training in the world. From boot camp to specialized combat training, Marines are prepared both mentally and physically to face the challenges of combat. This training instills confidence, discipline, and a strong sense of camaraderie among Marines, which contributes to their effectiveness in combat.

Marines are known for their ability to adapt and overcome in any situation. Whether fighting in the the jungles or the mountains of Vietnam, Marines are trained to be versatile and resourceful warriors who can thrive in diverse environments and under changing circumstances.

Marines are deeply committed to their mission and to the welfare of their fellow Marines. They understand the importance of teamwork, leadership, and selflessness in combat, and they are willing to make sacrifices to achieve their objectives and ensure the safety of their comrades.

Ethos of Semper Fidelis (Always Faithful): Semper Fidelis is more than just a motto for Marines; it's a way of life. Marines are taught to be loyal to their country, their Corps, and each other, no matter the circumstances. This sense of loyalty and fidelity fosters a strong bond among Marines and earns them the respect of their peers and leaders.

Above all else, Marines are taught to put the needs of others before their own. Whether on the battlefield or in peacetime, Marines are willing to go above and beyond the call of duty to serve their country and protect those in need. This selfless dedication to service earns them the admiration and respect of their fellow citizens.

The prestige and respect that United States Marines received for fighting in the Vietnam War was a reflection of their dedication, bravery, and commitment to duty. Marines are held in high esteem by their peers, their leaders, and the nation as a whole for their unwavering courage and sacrifice in defense of freedom and democracy.

Your book starts with a Marine's first insignias. It then walks you through Marine Corps rank insignia, combat and skill badges and medals and ribbons. Finally, as hard as we try, we know there will be mistakes in this book. Therefore please send all comments, suggestions and corrections in care of the publisher. Thank you for using this book. In so doing, you honor the memory of great Americans, our Marine Corps veterans. **"Let no veteran be forgotten!"**

Introduction to Marine Corps Insignia

The Marine Corps has great respect for everything and anything that enhances the uniqueness of the Corps and fosters the discipline, loyalty, courage, brotherhood and achievement that make the word "Marine" stand for the highest definition of military pride. The insignia of the Marine Corps are very much a part of this pride on display.

Marine Corps Emblem - displays a crested eagle above a globe of the Western Hemisphere backed by a fouled anchor. In the eagle's beak is a scroll emblazoned with the Latin motto of the Corps, *Semper Fidelis (Always Faithful)*. The Emblem of the Marine Corps was adopted in 1868 and was designed by Brigadier General Jacob Zeilin, the 7th Commandant.

Official Seal of the Marine Corps - consists of the traditional bronze Marine Corps Emblem, which is displayed on a scarlet background. The emblem is encircled with a navy blue band edged in a gold rope rim and inscribed Department of the Navy, United States Marine Corps in gold letters. The Official Seal of the Marine Corps was established on 22 June 1954 and was designed at the suggestion of General Lemuel C. Shepherd, Jr., the 20th Commandant.

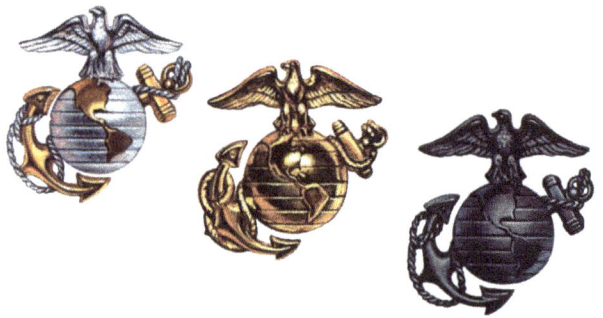

Branch of Service Insignia - is modeled after the Marine Corps Emblem, except without the motto scroll. This insignia is worn on the uniform cover, coat collars and lapels. The officers' dress insignia is gold and silver. The enlisted branch of service insignia is the same general design as the officers' insignia except the dress insignia is gold. The service insignia was bronze from World War II until June 1963 when the color was changed to non-glossy black. The service insignia for both officers and enlisted is currently non-glossy black.

Interestingly, officers have worn the insignia on their collars since the 1870's, but enlisted Marines didn't have this privilege until World War I, when Franklin D. Roosevelt, as Secretary of the Navy, directed them to wear insignia discs. This change was in recognition of the 4th Marine Brigade's victory at Belleau Wood. The eagle, globe and anchor insignia was approved for enlisted Marines in 1920. From 1941 to 1961, the collar device was also worn on the enlisted shirt collars (when coats were not worn). During this period the anchor on the insignia was not fouled with anchor cable.

Since the current insignia was standardized in 1936, manufacturers of Marine Corps insignia have been held to very tight contract specifications. There have been no changes in the current design for enlisted insignia since 1956 and officers since 1962. Marines refer to the insignia as the "Bird and Ball", or the "Globe and Anchor", but it is more properly called the "Eagle, Globe and Anchor."

The current officers' branch of service insignia for the dress/service cap consists of a view of the globe (Western Hemisphere) about 7/8 inch in diameter, intersected by a fouled anchor, and surmounted by an eagle. The rope of the fouled anchor is only connected at distinct points. The insignia is provided with a screwpost securely soldered to and projecting from the approximate center rear of the globe, and fitted with a milled nut. The dress insignia is gold and silver while the service insignia is finished in non-glossy black.

The design of the current officers' dress collar insignia is identical to the dress cap insignia, except that it is about 11/16 inch in diameter. The design of the officers' service collar insignia is identical to the service cap insignia, except that it is 9/16 inch in diameter.

Enlisted branch of service insignia is the same general design as officers' insignia, except that the rope is continuously connected to the fouled anchor of the emblem. Dress insignia is stamped of gold color metal while service insignia is stamped and finished in non-glossy black.

Uniform Buttons - come in gold and non glossy-black. The buttons display an eagle perched on top of a fouled anchor and thirteen stars surround the upper edge. The dress buttons are gold with a burnished rim, while the service uniform buttons are non-glossy black.

Necktie (field scarf) Clasp - is a lined stamped gold bar with a Marine Corps emblem on a centered gold disc; the officers' clasp has the emblem in silver, while the enlisted clasp has a gold emblem. The original clasp, worn in the mid to late '50's by both officers and enlisted, was non-glossy black. During the Vietnam period, as the width of civilian neckties narrowed, so did the width of the field scarf and the necktie clasp. No necktie clasp was worn During World War II and immediately following.

Honorable Service Lapel Pin (World War II Honorable Discharge Pin) - was a token of appreciation given to every American service member who was discharged during and after World War II for service between September 1939 and December 1946. The pin is a small gold-plated brass emblem 7/16 inch high by 5/8 inch wide. This "Badge of Service," nicknamed "Ruptured Duck," was designed by Anthony de Franisci for the War Department. The design consists of an eagle perched within a ring and is worn as a civilian suit lapel button. This same design was used as a cloth insignia (1-1/2 inches high by 3 inches wide for wear on the uniform) for all Marines who were permitted to wear their uniform after being discharged.

Honorable Discharge Lapel Pin - is a small gold-plated brass emblem 7/16 inch high by 5/8 inch wide. The design consists of a Marine Corps emblem in a circle with the words U.S. Marine Corps - Honorable Discharge. This pin is intended to be worn as a civilian suit lapel pin.

Retirement Lapel Pin - is a small plated emblem 7/16 inch high by 5/8 inch wide. The design consists of a Marine Corps emblem in a circle with the words U.S. Marine Corps - Retired. The pin is gold for twenty years service and silver for thirty. This pin is intended to be worn as a civilian suit lapel pin.

Gold Star Pin - is a small gold-plated brass emblem 7/16 inch high by 5/8 inch wide. The design consists of a gold star encircled by a laurel wreath. This pin is presented to the families of Marines killed in the line of duty and is intended to be worn as recognition of the appreciation of a grateful nation. The pin is also known as the "Gold Star Mothers" pin.

Officer Candidate Program Insignia - During World War II, and the two decades following, Marine Officer Candidates wore collar insignia identifying them as Officer Candidates (OC), Platoon Leaders Class (PLC) and Marine Air Cadets (MARCAD). Officer Candidates wore silver "OC" insignia; Platoon Leaders Class Candidates wore gold (Class 1) and silver (Class 2) "PLC" insignia; and Marine Aviation Cadets wore gold winged silver propellers. Marine Option NROTC Midshipmen wore no identifying collar insignia.

Service and Utility Uniform Insignia

Officer Service Insignia (1950's)  **Officer Service Insignia (Current)**  **Enlisted Service Insignia (Current)**

Service Buttons (Current)  **Officer Lapel Insignia (WWII)** 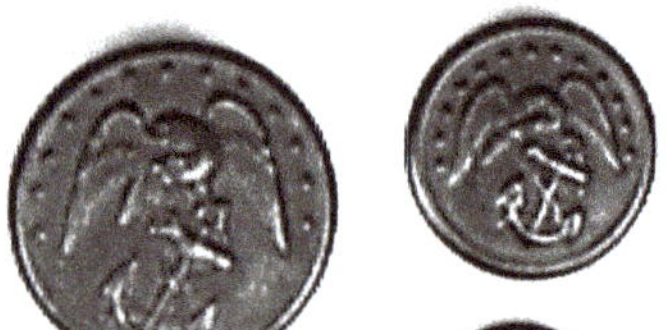  **Enlisted Service Buttons (1950's)**

EOD Utility Insignia  **Hospital Corpsman Utility Insignia**  **Dental Technician Utility Insignia**  **Marine Gunner Utility Insignia**

Sergeant Major Utility Insignia

Master Gunnery Sergeant Utility Insignia

First Sergeant Utility Insignia

Master Sergeant Utility Insignia

Gunnery Sergeant Utility Insignia

Staff Sergeant Utility Insignia

Sergeant Utility Insignia

Corporal Utility Insignia

Lance Corporal Utility Insignia

Private First Class Utility Insignia

Navy FMF Insignia

The Marine Corps, being a part of the Department of the Navy, receives its medical, dental and religious support from the Navy. *All the Insignia below would be black on uniforms.*

Hospital Corpsman

Religious Program Specialist

Dental Technician

Petty Officer 1st class

Petty Officer 2nd class

Petty Officer 3rd class

Enlisted Navy personnel attached to the Corps providing these services are authorized to wear Marine Corps service and utility uniforms, but wear their rank and corps insignia. On the service uniform the Navy rank and corps insignia is dark blue on green.

Chaplains

Christian

Jewish

Chaplains, medical and dental officers are also authorized to wear uniforms with their appropriate rank and corps insignia when serving with Marine units.

Officer Cover Insignia

Chief Petty Officer Cover Insignia

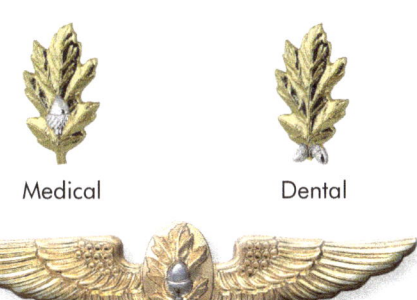
Medical   Dental

Flight Surgeon

Navy medical officers also serve Marine Air Wings as flight surgeons.

Fleet Marine Force Warfare Insignia (not authorized until 2000) Is a silver metal pin for enlisted and a gold pin for officers, with a Marine Corps eagle globe and anchor and crossed M-1 Garand rifles on a background of waves breaking on a beach. Below the emblem is a banner with the words "FLEET MARINE FORCE."

Eur.-African-Mid. East Campaign Medal

Asiatic-Pacific Campaign Medal

Korean Service Medal

Armed Forces Expeditionary Medal

Vietnam Service Medal

Navy personnel have served gallantly with the Corps over the years and are a part of its proud history. Those attached to the Marine Corps units who engage in active combat operations are entitled to wear a small Marine Corps emblem device on the ribbon of the appropriate campaign medal.

1970's Enlisted Cover Insignia
(still worn by female enlisted personnel)

Medals of America Press

Marine Corps Breast Insignia

Breast insignia are worn by Marines who are qualified/designated in selected areas. Breast insignia are worn on the left breast of all service and dress coats, and may be worn on khaki shirts or utility jackets when worn as an outer garment. Not more than two Marine Corps approved breast insignia are worn on the left, and not more than one foreign pilot or other U.S. service pilot /navigator insignia is worn on the right at a time. Miniature insignia, one-half regular size, are worn on evening dress jackets.

Naval Aviator Insignia - Bronze, gold-plated metal pin consisting of a fouled anchor surmounted by a shield, centered on the basic wings. The fouled anchor is 7/8 inch long. The height and width of the shield is 1/2 inch. The Naval Aviator Insignia is awarded to officers who have successfully completed an authorized course of instruction (Naval Flight School-Pensacola) as prescribed by the Commandant of the Marine Corps (CMC) or the Chief of Naval Operations (CNO).

Naval Flight Officer Insignia - Bronze, gold-plated metal pin consisting of two crossed fouled anchors surcharged with a shield, centered on the basic wings. The fouled anchors are 7/8 inch long. The height and width of the shield is 1/2 inch. The Naval Flight Officer Insignia is awarded to officers who have successfully completed an appropriate course of instruction as prescribed by the Commandant of the Marine Corps (CMC) or the Chief of Naval Operations (CNO).

Naval Astronaut (NFO) Insignia - A gold embroidered or gold metal winged pin with a star shooting diagonally from bottom right to top left through an elliptical ring, on the shield of the traditional Naval Flight Officer's wings. The badge is issued to Naval Flight Officers who have completed astronaut training at NASA and have subsequently participated in a space flight more than 50 miles above the Earth.

Naval Astronaut Insignia - Bronze, gold-plated wings of a Naval Aviator or Naval Flight Officer with a shooting star and ring superimposed upon the center shield. A Marine designated by the CMC as a Naval Astronaut (pilot, NFO, or mission specialist) wears the Naval Astronaut Insignia.

Marine Aerial Navigator Insignia (1945-1947)- Bronze, gold-plated metal pin consisting of the basic wings with a central device of two fouled anchors surmounted by a replica of a mariner's compass, superimposed on a silver-colored disk. The fouled anchors are 5/8 inch long; diameter of the disk, 1/2 inch; diameter of the compass, 3/8 inch. The Marine Aerial Navigator Insignia is awarded to Marine officers and enlisted personnel who have successfully completed an appropriate course of instruction as prescribed by the Military Occupational Specialty (MOS) manual. The Insignia was instituted in 1945 as the "Naval Aviation Observers (Navigation) Insignia, and abolished in March 1947 and replaced by the naval Aviation Observers Insignia.

Naval Aviation Observer Insignia - Bronze, gold-plated metal pin consisting of the basic wings with a central device of an "O" circumscribing an erect plain anchor, both in silver in bold relief, the center of the "O" being filled with gold. The outer diameter of the "O" is 3/4 inch; inner diameter, 9/16 inch; height of the anchor, 1/2 inch. The Naval Aviation Observer Insignia is awarded to individuals who have successfully completed an appropriate course of instruction as prescribed by Headquarters Marine Corps (HQMC) and accumulated 200 hours of flight time directly related to the specified aerial duty. At one time this insignia was also awarded to Marines who are now authorized to wear the Naval Aircrew Insignia.

Naval Aircrew Insignia - Bronze, gold-plated metal pin consisting of the basic wings with a circular center design and anchor with the block letters "AC" superimposed. The circle diameter is 3/4 inch; anchor height is 1/2 inch. The Naval Aircrew Insignia is awarded to naval aircrewmen who have completed a locally administered course of instruction and are assigned as flight aircrew members. Assignments include: Helicopter crewchiefs, airborne electronic countermeasures operators, airborne radio operators and VG jet aircraft flight engineers.

Combat Aircrew Insignia - Oxidized silver-colored, winged metal pin, with a gold-colored circular shield with a superimposed fouled anchor; the word "AIRCREW" in raised letters on a silver-colored background below the circular shield; above the shield is a silver-colored scroll; the insignia measures two inches from wing tip to wing tip; circle on the shield, 5/16 inch in diameter. Gold stars, up to a total of three, as merited, are mounted on the scroll, necessary holes being pierced to receive them. The Combat Aircrew Insignia is awarded to aircrewmen who have participated in aerial flight during combat, and those enlisted personnel who qualify for nontechnical aircrew positions and serve in such positions in aerial combat. The Marine must be a volunteer and a regularly assigned member of a flight crew onboard a Marine aircraft participating in combat operations. The Marine must also be a graduate of an established course of instruction and/or OJT qualifying him for a position in the flight crew of a Marine aircraft. Combat aircrewmen who have qualified to wear combat stars may wear the Combat Aircrew Insignia on a permanent basis. A maximum of three combat stars may be awarded for display on the Combat Aircrew Insignia. The criteria for earning individual combat stars are as follows:

a. Engagement of an enemy aircraft.
b. Engagement of an enemy vessel with bombs, rockets, torpedoes, guns or missiles.
c. Participation in offensive or defensive operations against enemy fortified positions.

A Marine who is qualified to wear the Naval Aircrew Insignia and the Combat Aircrew Insignia has the option of wearing the one of his choice.

Basic Parachutist Insignia - Oxidized silver pin about 1-1/2 inches long and 3/4 inch high, consisting of an open parachute flanked on either side by wings curving up and inward so that the tips join the edge of the parachute canopy. The Basic Parachutist Insignia is an Army insignia, but is awarded to Marine officers and enlisted personnel who have successfully completed a CG MCCDC (WF11B) approved parachuting course (i.e.: the Army Airborne School at Fort Benning, Georgia).

Navy /Marine Corps Parachutist Insignia - Bronze, gold-plated metal pin consisting of the basic aviation wings with a gold-colored open parachute centered on the wings. The parachute is inch wide at its widest part and 13/16 inch long from top to bottom. The Navy/Marine Corps Parachutist Insignia is awarded to Marine officers and enlisted personnel who have completed a CG MCCDC (WF11B) approved parachuting course, and completed five <u>additional</u> parachute jumps. The additional jumps must include at least one combat equipment day jump and two combat equipment night jumps. The additional jumps must also employ two or more types of military aircraft.

Basic Explosive Ordnance Disposal (EOD) Insignia - Oxidized silver pin consisting of a 1-inch high shield with a conventional drop bomb, point down, and four lightning bolts, all in front of a laurel leaf wreath 1-3/4 inches wide. The Basic EOD Insignia is awarded to Marine officers and enlisted personnel in accordance with MCO 3571.2 (Criteria for Basic, Senior, and Master EOD). The Marine must have successfully completed the basic EOD course taught at the US Naval EOD School, Indian Head, Maryland and be assigned to a position for which the course is a prerequisite. The wreath of the insignia symbolizes the achievements and laurels gained by EOD personnel. The bomb design is copied from the design of the World War II Bomb Disposal Badge and its three fins represent the major areas of nuclear, conventional and chemical/biological interests. The lightening bolts symbolize the potential destructive power and the courage and professionalism of the EOD personnel. The shield represents the EOD mission to prevent a detonation and protect personnel and property.

Marine Corps Breast Insignia

Senior Explosive Ordnance Disposal (EOD) Insignia - The same as the Basic EOD insignia, but with a 7/32 inch star on the drop bomb. The Senior EOD Insignia is awarded to Marine personnel in accordance with MCO 3571.2 (Criteria for Basic, Senior, and Master EOD). The Marine must have served in an EOD position for at least 36 months cumulative service following the award of the Basic EOD Insignia.

Master Explosive Ordnance Disposal (EOD) Insignia - The same as the Senior EOD insignia with a star in a laurel wreath above the shield. The Master EOD Insignia is awarded to Marine personnel in accordance with MCO 3571.2 (Criteria for Basic, Senior, and Master EOD). The Marine must have been awarded the Senior EOD Insignia, have at least 60 months cumulative service in an EOD position, and have been recommended by his immediate commander.

SCUBA Diver Insignia - Oxidized silver pin approximately 1-1/16 inches high, one inch wide, consisting of wet suit headgear and face mask with breathing apparatus around the neck. The SCUBA Diver Insignia is awarded to Marine officers and enlisted personnel who have completed a CG MCCDC (WF11B) approved underwater diving course.

Second Class Diver Insignia - Oxidized silver MK5 diving helmet pin approximately 1-1/16 inches high, one inch wide. The insignia is awarded for basic deep sea dive qualifications.

First Class Diver Insignia - Oxidized silver MK5 diving helmet pin approximately 1-1/16 inches high, one inch wide. The insignia is awarded for deep sea dive qualifications. The badge includes the design of the diver's helmet to reflect diving operations and the dolphins suggest the function of diving, without the helmet of a deep sea diver.

Master Diver Insignia - Oxidized silver MK5 diving helmet pin approximately 1-1/16 inches high, one inch wide. The trident is added to the design of the First class badge and is symbolic of a Marine spearhead and stands for valor and strength. The insignia is awarded for deep sea dive qualifications and issued in the degrees of Second Class, First Class, Master Diver, and Diving Medical Technician for medical personnel who have qualified as both divers and medical response personnel to medical emergencies underwater. The diving medical officer and the diving medical technician insignia are awarded to naval medical personnel qualified as divers or medical technicians, respectively. The diving medical insignia resembles the master diver insignia, but is decorated with a caduceus. Officer Master Diver badges badges are issued in gold color.

Marine Corps Officer Rank Insignia

The Marine Corps officers' grade structure follows the other U.S. military services and uses the same rank structure as the Army and the Air Force. It should be noted that the rank insignia, although similar in appearance to the other services, has its own unique peculiarities (e.g.: the captain's and lieutenant's bars do not have a beveled edge, etc.)

The Officer grades in order of seniority are:

Rank	Pay Grade
General	O-10
Lieutenant General	O-9
Major General	O-8
Brigadier General	O-7
Colonel	O-6
Lieutenant Colonel	O-5
Major	O-4
Captain	O-3
First Lieutenant	O-2
Second Lieutenant	O-1
Chief Warrant Officer, CWO5	W-5
Chief Warrant Officer, CWO4	W-4
Chief Warrant Officer, CWO3	W-3
Chief Warrant Officer, CWO2	W-2
Warrant Officer, WO1	W-1
Marine Gunner	W-5 thru W-1

Officer rank insignia are worn on both epaulets of dress and service coats, as well as both collars of shirts and field and utility coats.

General Rank Insignia - Four silver-colored, five-pointed, stars. Shoulder stars are one inch in diameter and are either fastened together on a metal holding bar or placed individually with one point of each star in the same line; distance between the centers of adjacent stars is 3/4 inch. Collar stars are 9/16 inch in diameter and are fastened together on a metal holding bar in a straight line with one ray of each star pointing upward and at right angles to the holding bar.

Lieutenant General Rank Insignia - Three silver-colored stars, of the same type and arranged in the same manner as for a general, except the distance between centers of adjacent shoulder stars is one inch.

Major General Rank Insignia - Two silver-colored stars of the same type and arranged in the same manner as for a lieutenant general.

Brigadier General Rank Insignia - One silver-colored star.

Colonel Rank Insignia - A silver-colored spread eagle, right and left talons of one foot grasping an olive branch, the other, a bundle of arrows. Shoulder insignia; slightly curved, with 1-1/2-inch wing span. Collar insignia; flat, with 31/32 inch wing span.

Lieutenant Colonel Rank Insignia - A seven-pointed, silver-colored oak leaf, raised and veined. Shoulder insignia; slightly curved, one inch from stem tip to center leaf tip. Collar insignia: flat, 23/32 inch from stem tip to center leaf tip.

Major Rank Insignia - A seven-pointed, gold-colored oak leaf, raised and veined. Shoulder insignia; slightly curved, one inch from stem tip to center leaf tip. Collar insignia: flat, 23/32 inch from stem tip to center leaf tip.

Captain Rank Insignia - Two smooth silver-colored bars, without bevel, attached at each end by a holding bar. Shoulder insignia: each bar slightly curved, 1-1/8 inches long by 3/8 inch wide, and 3/8 inch apart. Collar insignia; flat, each bar 3/4 inch long by 1/4 inch wide and 1/4 inch apart.

First Lieutenant Rank Insignia - One silver-colored bar of the same type as for a captain.

Second Lieutenant Rank Insignia - One gold-colored bar of the same type as for a first lieutenant

Chief Warrant Officer, CWO5 Rank Insignia - One silver-colored bar of the same type as for a first lieutenant with one scarlet enamel stripe superimposed lengthwise. Shoulder insignia; center enamel stripe is 1/8 inch wide and 1-1/8 inch long. Collar insignia; center enamel stripe is 1/8 inch wide and 3/4 inch long.

Chief Warrant Officer, CWO4 Rank Insignia - One silver-colored bar of the same type as for a first lieutenant with three scarlet enamel blocks superimposed. Shoulder insignia; center enamel block is 1/4 inch wide, with 1/8 inch wide outer blocks, 1/4 inch from the edges of the center block. Collar insignia; center enamel block is 5/32 inch wide, with 3/32 inch wide outer blocks, 5/32 inch from the edges of the center block.

Chief Warrant Officer, CWO3 Rank Insignia - One silver-colored bar of the same type as for a CWO-4 with two scarlet enamel blocks superimposed. Shoulder insignia blocks are 3/8 inch wide and 1/4 inch apart. Collar insignia; blocks are 1/4 inch wide and 5/32 inch apart.

Chief Warrant Officer, CWO2 Rank Insignia - One gold-colored bar of the same type as for a second lieutenant with three scarlet enamel blocks arranged in the same manner as for a CWO-4.

Warrant Officer, WO1 Rank Insignia - One gold-colored bar of the same type as for a CWO-2 with two scarlet enamel blocks arranged in the same manner as for a CWO-3

Marine Gunner Insignia - One gold-colored replica of a bursting bomb (dress), one non-glossy black replica of a bursting bomb (service). Shoulder insignia; overall height of the bomb is about 1-1/4 inches. Collar insignia; flat, overall height of about 3/4 inch.

Evening Dress Sleeve Ornamentation

General Officers

Field Officers

Company Officers — Female Officers

(Marine Corps Art Collection)

Medals of America Press 15

Marine Corps Enlisted Rank and Service Insignia

The current Marine Corps enlisted grades in seniority are:

Rank	Pay Grade
Sergeant Major of the Marine Corps	E-9
Sergeant Major (Master Gunnery Sergeant)	E-9
First Sergeant (Master Sergeant)	E-8
Gunnery Sergeant	E-7
Staff Sergeant	E-6
Sergeant	E-5
Corporal	E-4
Lance Corporal	E-3
Private First Class	E-2
Private	E-1

First Sergeant — Master Gunnery Sergeant — Sergeant Major

Staff Sergeant (Sleeve) — Staff Sergeant (Collar)

The Marine Corps currently uses four types of rank insignia (chevrons): gold on red for the dress blue uniform (blues), green on red for the service uniform (greens), green on khaki for the service shirt and black metal on utilities (Women Marines wore green on white chevrons between 1952 and 1979 on the old green and white summer service uniform). Enlisted rank insignia was worn on both sleeves of dress and service coats, jackets, and shirts as well as both collars of field and utility coats. The practice of using black metal collar rank insignia was also adopted after the Korean War and has been used on utilities collars since.

In 1959, a new rank structure was approved which brought back the old Lance Corporal rank, added crossed rifles to the enlisted rank insignia and differentiated rank insignia between command and technical responsibilities at the E-8 and E-9, pay grades. The Lance Corporal rank replaced the old E-3 Corporal and "lifted" the balance of the rank structure as shown on page 17. The earlier addition of the E-8 and E-9, pay grades allowed senior Staff NCO's rank insignia to show those with command and personnel responsibilities as First Sergeant and Sergeant Major with a diamond and star respectively, and those with technical responsibilities as Master Sergeant and Master Gunnery Sergeant with crossed rifles and a bursting bomb.

Staff Sergeant

Marine Band Musician

8 Years Service — 4 Years Service

Staff non commissioned officers currently wear an 1890's style insignia on SNCO's evening dress jacket. This insignia is gold on scarlet.

Musicians in the Marine Band (The President's Own) currently wear rank insignia (E-6 to E-9) similar to their regular counterparts, except that the insignia contains a musical lyre rather than crossed rifles.

Enlistment, or service stripes, are worn on dress and service jackets, one for each four years of service. Service stripes are gold on red for the dress blue uniform (blues), green on red for the service uniform (greens). During the late 1950's and early 1960's, service stripes were available green on khaki for the old Summer Service Coats (khaki), which was an optional uniform for Staff NCO's.

Lance Corporal — Master Sergeant

(Marine Corps Art Collection)

Enlisted Rank Structure

1944-1946		1946-1958		1958-PRESENT	
RANK	INSIGNIA	RANK	INSIGNIA	RANK	INSIGNIA
		SGTMAJ		1. SGTMAJMC 2. SGTMAJ 3. MGYSGT	1. 2. 3.
		1stSGT		1. 1stSGT 2. MSGT	1. 2.
1. SGTMAJ 1st SGT 2. MGYSGT MTSGT QMSGT PMSGT	1 2	MSGT		GYSGT	
1. GYSGT 2. TECHSGT	1 2	TECHSGT		SSGT	
1. PLTSGT 2. SSGT	1 2	SSGT		SGT	
SGT		SGT		CPL	
CPL		CPL		LC PL	
PFC		PFC		PFC	
PVT		PVT		PVT	

Medals of America Press

Marine Corps Service/Identification Badges

The Presidential Service Badge (PSB), Vice Presidential Service Badge (VPSB), Office of the Secretary of Defense Identification Badge (OSD ID Badge), and Joint Chiefs of Staff Identification Badge (JCS ID Badge) are authorized to be worn on Marine Corps uniforms and can be worn after detachment from qualifying duty.

Marines assigned to joint/unified commands may also be authorized to wear distinctive command identification badges, but only upon approval from the CMC (MCUB). Approved command identification devices are worn for the duration of assignment to that command only.

Presidential Service Badge (PSB)

USMC Photo

The Presidential Service Badge was established on 1 September 1964. It replaced the White House Service Badge, which had been established on 1 June 1960. The badge is given by the President to members of the Armed Forces assigned to duty in the White House or to military units and support facilities under the administration of the Military Assistant to the President for a period of at least one year, after 20 January 1961, as recognition, in a permanent way, of their contribution in the service of the President. Once earned, the badge becomes a permanent part of the recipient's uniform and may be worn after the recipient leaves presidential service. The PSB consists of a blue enameled disc, 1-15/16 inches in diameter, surrounded by 27 gold rays radiating from the center. Superimposed on the disc is a gold-colored device taken from the seal of the President of the United States, encircled with 50 stars.

Vice Presidential Service Badge
(VPSB)
(new)

Vice Presidential Service Badge (VPSB)

Vice Presidential
Service Badge (VPSB)
(old)

The Vice Presidential Service Badge was established on 8 July 1970. The badge is awarded in the name of the Vice President to members of the Armed Forces who have been assigned to duty in the Office of the Vice President for a period of at least one-year after 20 January 1969. The first VPSB was 1-15/16 inches overall with a white enameled disc and satin gold rays along its edge. In the center was a gold eagle with drooping wings surrounded by 50 gold stars. The current VPSB consists of a white enameled disc, 1-15/16 inches in diameter surrounded by 27 gold rays radiating from the center. Superimposed on the disc is a gold-colored device taken from the seal of the Vice President of the United States. Once earned, the badge becomes a permanent part of the uniform.

Full Size

Miniature

Office of the Secretary of Defense Identification Badge (OSD ID)

The Office of the Secretary of Defense Identification Badge is worn by personnel who are assigned on a permanent basis to the following organizational elements:

1. Office of the Secretary and Deputy Secretary of Defense.
2. Offices of the Under Secretaries of Defense.
3. Offices of the Assistant Secretaries of Defense.
4. Office of the General Counsel of the Department of Defense.
5. Offices of the Assistants to the Secretary of Defense.
6. Office of the Defense Advisor, US Mission to the North Atlantic Treaty Organization (NATO).

After completion of one year of duty, the individual is entitled to permanent possession of the badge. A member of the Reserve Components who is assigned an authorized Reserve Forces position in OSD for a period of no less than two years, on or after 1 January 1973, is entitled to permanent possession of the badge. The OSD ID badge consists of an eagle with wings displayed horizontally, grasping three crossed gold arrows, and having on its breast an enameled shield consisting of a blue upper portion and 13 alternating red and white stripes on the lower portion; a gold ring passing behind the wing tips bearing 13 gold stars above the eagle and a wreath of laurel and olive in green enamel below the eagle; all superimposed on a silver sunburst of 33 rays two inches in diameter.

Full Size

Miniature

USMC Photo

Joint Chiefs of Staff Identification Badge (JCS ID)

The Joint Chiefs of Staff Identification Badge is awarded to military personnel who have been assigned to duty and served not less than one year after 13 January 1961, in a position of responsibility under the direct cognizance of the Joint Chiefs of Staff. The award of the badge must be approved by the Chairman, Joint Chiefs of Staff; the head of a Directorate of the Joint Staff; or one of the subordinate agencies of the Organization of the Joint Chiefs of Staff. Personnel are authorized to wear the badge following reassignment from duty with the JCS.

The standard size JCS ID badge consists of the United States shield (upper portion in blue, and 13 stripes of alternating red and white enamel) superimposed on four gold metal unsheathed swords (two placed vertically and two diagonally), pointing to the top, with points and pommels resting on the wreath, blades and grips entwined with a gold metal continuous scroll surrounding the shield with the word "JOINT" at the top and the words "CHIEFS OF STAFF" at bottom, in blue enamel letters; all within an oval silver metal wreath of laurel 2-1/4 inches high by two inches wide.

Marine Corps Service/Identification Badges

During Vietnam War, Marine Corps military police battalions were reactivated for the first time. On 28 May 1966, the 1st Military Police Battalion arrived at Da Nang, South Vietnam and relieved the 3rd Battalion, 3rd Marines from responsibility for the security of Da Nang Air Base. The 3rd MP Battalion scout dog patroled near Marble Mountain in 1968 and the 1st MP Battalion guarded the main bridges into Da Nang in 1969.

By 1968, the 3rd Military Police Battalion had joined the 1st MP Battalion at Da Nang and both units were under the control of Force Logistic Command/1st Force Service Regiment which provided logistic support to the 1st Marine Division and the South Korean 2nd Marine Brigade. The 3rd MP Battalion operated the III MAF brig in Da Nang built to hold 200 prisoners. The 3rd MP Battalion furnished war dogs for the 1st Marine Division, staffed the III MAF Criminal Investigation Department and contributed a 50-man MP contingent to the U.S. Armed Forces Police (AFP) in Da Nang. Marines from this AFP detachment protected the U.S. Consulate in Da Nang and helped guard the POW ward at the U.S. Army's 95th Evacuation Hospital. Until 1 January 1970, the commander of the 3rd MP Battalion had the additional duty of III MAF Provost Marshal. The 1st and 3rd MP Battalions fought in the defense of the Da Nang Vital Area in the Tet and Phase III offensives of 1968 and the Tet 1969 attacks.

In early 1971, the 1st MP Battalion was based at Camp Stokes near Da Nang Air Base. On 7 May 1971, with the cessation of all Marine combat in South Vietnam, the battalion ended small-unit operations and turned defense of Da Nang Air Base over to the Army of the Republic of Vietnam 104th Regional Force Battalion and the 796th Regional Force Company. The battalion retained its AFP and brig duties throughout the rest of May, as well as guarding the remaining 3rd Marine Amphibious Brigade cantonments. On 5 June the battalion was released from all AFP tasks and the battalion stood down on 7 June. By 24 June all elements had departed for Camp Pendleton, where the battalion was deactivated.

United States Marine Corps Military Police Badge

Marines serving in the Military Police Occupational Specialty (MOS 5811) are law enforcement officers with jurisdiction on and around military installations. They are esponsible for the security, safety, and daily admission onto military bases.

Marine Corps Military Police Corrections Badge

A Marine Corps Corrections Specialist is a sub MOS of the Military Police and Correctional field, and helps the Commander of their unit by enforcing and upholding the law. They are responsible for preserving military order and control.

United States Marine Corps Criminal Investigation Division (USMC C.I.D.) Badge

CID Agents are a federal law enforcement agency that investigates crimes against persons and property within the United States Marine Corps. They are an enlisted active duty Marines between the grades of E-5 through E-9 or WO1 to CWO5.

Marine Corps Marksmanship Badges

Rifle Expert

Rifle Sharpshooter

Rifle Marksman

In July of 1958, the Marine Corps adopted the current series of marksmanship badges. The regulations called for three awards for both rifle and pistol with the addition of new requalification bars for both rifle and pistol.

Wording changed from "EXPERT RIFLEMAN" to "RIFLE EXPERT" and Crossed M-1 rifles replaced the M1903 rifles on the Expert badge.

The Sharpshooter badge was modified also, with a new bar with the word "RIFLE SHARPSHOOTER", and the target in the center of the Maltese cross was eliminated in favor of the Marine Corps emblem.

A square three ring target suspended from a bar with the words "RIFLE MARKSMAN" replaced the old Marksman badge.

Pistol Expert

Pistol Sharpshooter

Pistol Marksman

The Pistol Expert badge is similar to the Rifle Expert badge having a wreath on which two crossed M1911A1 pistols are superimposed. The Pistol Sharpshooter and Marksman badges are simply smaller versions of their rifle award counterparts and read "PISTOL" rather than "RIFLE".

During the course of this century, badges and qualification rules have changed, but the excellence in marksmanship still remains a major emphasis in the Corps.

Medals of America Press

Marine Corps Marksmanship and Trophy Badges

Listed and illustrated as follows in order of precedence, are the marksmanship awards authorized for wear on the Marine Corps uniform.

Distinguished International Shooter

Distinguished Marksman

Distinguished Pistol Shot

Lauchheimer Trophy *(Silver)*

Rifle Championship *(McDaugal Trophy)*

Pistol Championship *(Walsh Trophy)*

National, Interservice, & Marine Corps Rifle Competition *(Bronze)*

National, Interservice, & Marine Corps Pistol Competition *(Gold)*

Inter-Division Rifle Team

Inter-Division Pistol Team

FMF Combat Infantry Trophy

Annual Rifle Squad Practice *(Silver)*

Division Rifle Competition *(Silver)*

Division Pistol Competition *(Bronze)*

Rifle Team Match *(Elliott Trophy)*

Pistol Team Match *(Edson Trophy)*

Aiguillettes, Breastcords, Shoulder Cords & Fourragere

Aiguillettes - Aides de Camp

Aiguillettes are worn by Marine officers to identify them as aides to top-ranking government officials and general officers. Aiguillettes are worn with both service and dress uniforms. Aiguillettes are worn on the right shoulder by aides to the President, Vice-President, foreign heads of state, and White House aides. All others wear the aiguillettes on the left shoulder.

Dress Aiguillettes

Dress aiguillettes are of round gold cord 1/4 inch in diameter, with a core of yellow cotton covered with gold or gilt thread. They consist of two cords made in three plaits, with a pencil attachment on the end of each plaited cord, and of two loops of single cord. The pencil attachment is gold-plated brass, 3.015 inches long, the cap is 0.656 inches long, and the pencil is 2.359 inches long. The cap has six leaves; the pencil has two miniature Marine Corps emblems (omitting motto ribbon and anchor rope) on the upper part and two wreaths on the lower part, all in relief around the circumference. The smooth surfaces are polished; the cap or upper part is stamped; and the lower part hollow-cast, turned, milled, and knurled.

Dress aiguillettes are the same regardless of the rank of the individual being served.

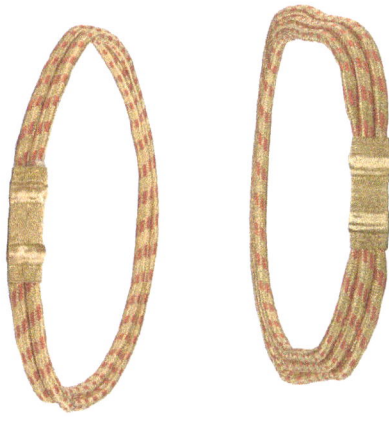

Service Aiguillettes

Service aiguillettes are of round gold wire and scarlet cord, 1/4 inch in diameter, and consist of two, three, or four loops sewn together all the way around. Service aiguillettes consist of loops which indicate:

Four Loops - Personal aides to the President or Vice President; aides at the White House; aides to the Secretary or Deputy Secretary of Defense, Secretary or Under Secretary of the Navy, and Assistant Secretaries of Defense or the Navy; aide to the General Counsel of the Navy; and naval attaches and assistant attaches assigned to an embassy.

Four Loops - Aides to generals, admirals, or officials of higher grade.

Three Loops - Aides to lieutenant generals and vice admirals.

Two Loops - Aides to major/brigadier generals, rear admirals, or other officers of lower grade entitled to an aide.

Two Loops - Officers appointed as aides to a governor of a state or territory may wear aiguillettes on official occasions.

Musician - Marine Band (President's Own)
(USMC Photo)

Bugler - Marine Drum & Bugle Corps
(Commandant's Own)

(Marine Corps Art Collection)

Aiguillettes - Marine Band

Aiguillettes are also worn on the full dress uniforms by members of the Marine Band. Gold plaited aiguillettes are worn by officers, while enlisted members wear white braid aiguillettes. These aiguillettes are worn from the left shoulder knot with cords worn in front of the arm and the loop suspended from the center top button of the coat.

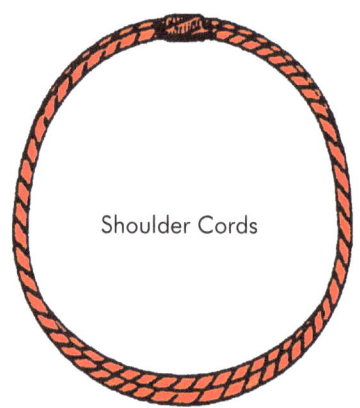

Shoulder Cords

Shoulder Cords - Female Drill Instructors

Shoulder cords were worn by female drill instructors at MCRD, Parris Island from November 1984 until October 1996, replacing cloth epaulets worn from 1969 to 1984. The cords were scarlet and worn on the left shoulder of both service and utility uniform. These cords were referred to by many DI's as "the big Irish pennant," in October 1996, the cords were retired when female drill instructors were authorized to wear the same field hat (campaign cover) worn by male drill instructors.

Breastcords - Marine Drum & Bugle Corps

Scarlet and gold breastcords are worn on the dress and service uniforms by members of the Marine Drum & Bugle Corps. These cords are worn when prescribed by the commander, but not on the utility uniform. The cords are worn from the left shoulder. Scarlet and gold breastcords are also worn on the dress uniforms by enlisted Marines on duty at the White House. The cords are worn from the left shoulder.

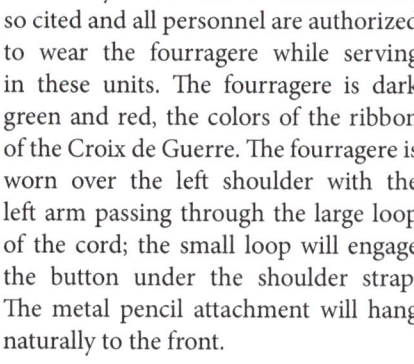

Fourragere

The fourragere was awarded by the French Ministry of War, during World War I, to units which were cited two or more times in the French Orders of the Army. The 5th and 6th Marines were so cited and all personnel are authorized to wear the fourragere while serving in these units. The fourragere is dark green and red, the colors of the ribbon of the Croix de Guerre. The fourragere is worn over the left shoulder with the left arm passing through the large loop of the cord; the small loop will engage the button under the shoulder strap. The metal pencil attachment will hang naturally to the front.

Fourragere

Marine Corps Shoulder Patches

Shown to the right are examples of both official and unofficial patches used by Marine Corps units during the Vietnam War.

The Marine Corps authorized the wearing of shoulder patches, properly called shoulder insignia, first during World War I and then again in March 1943, when LOI No. 372 authorized insignia for the 1st, 2nd, and 3rd Divisions, aircraft wings, and certain other specified units. They were worn on the left sleeve of service coats and overcoats. During the latter part of World War II nearly every Marine wore a shoulder patch identifying his unit. Initially these patches were referred to as "battle blazes" and were intended to commemorate battles fought by the unit; the 1st Division designed their shoulder patch with the title "Guadalcanal". Most of these patches identified the number associated with the unit, but the 1st Division was the only unit to include the name of an actual battle in the design.

These distinctive designs were not only used as uniform shoulder patches, but were also used during World War II on signs, letter heads, and shooting jacket emblems, etc. This practice was short-lived after the war however, since the practice of wearing shoulder patches on uniforms was abolished on 23 September 1947 (effective 1 January 1948). These uniform shoulder insignia were abolished on the grounds that the Marine Corps is a unified body organized to fight as a whole and individual shoulder patches did not reflect the spirit of the Corps.

During the Korean Conflict these designs unofficially reappeared as unit signs, but not on uniforms. In 1956 Headquarters Marine Corps re-thought the policy and approved the use of organizational distinguishing marks on everything but uniforms (the exception being G-1 flight jackets and flight suits). Because of this change in policy the practice of using patches accelerated during the Viet Nam era and is alive and well today. Many of these patches and others referred to as "novelty patches" were derived from those used in World War II and are too numerous for reproduction in this publication.

The "Guadalcanal Blaze" of the 1st Marine Division was the first Divisional Patch created during World War II and was designed by Lt. Col. M.B. Twining who served as the G-3 (Operations) during the Guadalcanal campaign. The badge shows the numeral one inscribed with the name "Guadalcanal" on a blue background.

1st Marine Division

FMF Pacific HQ.

1st Marine Division

3rd Marine Division

1st Marine Regiment (unoffical)

3rd Marine Regiment (unoffical)

4th Marine Regiment (unoffical)

5th Marine Regiment (unoffical)

7th Marine Regiment (unoffical)

9th Marine Regiment (unoffical)

11th Marine Regiment (unoffical)

12th Marine Regt. (unoffical)

26th Marine Regt. (unoffical)

South Vietnamese Marine Corps Patch

Marine Corps Awards and Decorations

The United States Marine Corps, being part of the Department of the Navy, follows the same awards program as the United States Navy. The awards program is governed by the Department of the Navy, but administered by the Corps. Most of the awards and decorations are the same for both the Navy and Marine Corps and some are common to all services.

Marine Corps awards fall into three classifications: personal and unit decorations, campaign and service medals, and marksmanship badges and trophies.

Marksmanship badges and trophies are awarded to individuals who demonstrate a proficiency or skill with a specific weapon during a specified practice exercise, competition or match. Marksmanship badges are worn to indicate an individual's ability with a specific weapon and are awarded in three levels: Expert, Sharpshooter and Marksman. Trophies are awarded at various levels to include: United States and international distinguished shooter competitions, Marine Corps rifle and pistol championships, national trophies for rifle and pistol, inter-service rifle and pistol matches, regional practices, combat exercises, division and inter-division contests.

Decoration - An award conferred on an individual for a specific act of gallantry or for meritorious service. Personal awards are conferred upon individuals for acts of heroism, acts of gallantry, or for meritorious service.

Badge - An award to an individual for some special proficiency or skill, which consists of a medallion suspended from a bar or bars.

Unit Award - An award made to an operating unit for outstanding performance and worn only by members of that unit who participated in the cited action.

The Marine Corps also participates with the other services in a system by which entire units are recognized for outstanding performance. Members of cited units are entitled to wear the appropriate award *(e.g.: Navy Presidential Unit Citation and Navy Unit Commendation, etc.)*.

Miniature Medal - A replica of a standard size medal, made to one-half original scale. Foreign medal miniatures will not exceed the size of American miniatures. The Medal of Honor will not be worn in miniature.

Ribbon Bar - A portion of the suspension ribbon of a medal, worn in lieu of the medal. Ribbon bars are also authorized for certain awards which have no medals.

Service Award - An award made to those who have participated in designated wars, campaigns, expeditions, etc., or who have fulfilled specified service requirements.

Rosette - Lapel device made by gathering the suspension ribbon of the medal into a circular shape.

Lapel Pin - A miniature enameled replica of the ribbon bar.

Attachment - Any appurtenance such as a star, clasp, or other device worn on a suspension ribbon of a medal or on the ribbon bar (also called device).

Decoration   Service Medal

The terms "decoration" and "medal" are used almost interchangeably today (as they are in this book), but there are recognizable distinctions between them. Decorations, are awarded for acts of gallantry and meritorious service and usually have distinctive (and often unique) shapes such as crosses or stars (there are exceptions to this, such as the Navy DSM, which is round). Medals are awarded for good conduct, participation in a particular campaign or expedition, or a noncombatant service and normally come in a round shape.

The fact that some very prestigious awards have the word "medal" in their titles (e.g.: Medal of Honor, Marine Corps Brevet Medal, Navy and Marine Corps Medal, etc.) can cause some confusion.

There are three different forms of medals (and decorations) for wear on the uniform: the full size medal, the miniature medal and the ribbon bar. The wearing of medals on the uniform is covered in the section "Wearing Medals, Ribbons, Badges and Insignia". The miniature medal, the enameled lapel button or pin and the civilian hatpin may be worn on civilian clothing,

Small metal attachments or devices are worn on the medal suspension ribbon and ribbon bar to denote additional awards, campaigns or subsequent service. These attachments come in the form of ★ stars, 🍂 oak leaf clusters, 3 numerals, E letters, etc. The attachments and manner of placement are described in detail in the section "Attachments and Devices" section.

Medals of America Press 27

Marine Corps' Vietnam Campaign Medals

National Defense Service Medal

Armed Forces Expeditionary Medal

Vietnam Service Medal

RVN Campaign Medal

RVN Gallantry Cross Unit Citation

The first American advisors in the Republic of South Vietnam were awarded the new Armed Forces Expeditionary Medal which was created in 1961 to cover campaigns for which no specific medal was instituted.

However, as the U.S. involvement in the Vietnamese conflict grew, a unique award, the Vietnam Service Medal was authorized, thus giving previous Marine recipients of the Expeditionary Medal the option of which medal to accept. The Government also authorized the acceptance of the Republic of Vietnam Campaign Medal for six months service in-country, or in the surrounding waters or the air after 1960. Towards the end of the war, a blanket general order authorized the RVN Gallantry Cross Unit Citation for all military personnel who served in Vietnam.

The most notable change in medal policy occurred during the Vietnam War when the Department of Defense authorized the large scale acceptance of South Vietnamese awards. The South Vietnamese Armed Forces had a comprehensive awards system built to reflect their past as a former French colony. Since a large number of American military advisors and special forces worked with the South Vietnamese Armed Forces for more than 15 years, (many serving multiple tours) numerous medals for valor and service were presented to U.S. personnel. Some of the most awarded were the Vietnamese Cross of Gallantry (for valor), the Civil Actions Medal and the Armed Forces Honor Medal (meritorious service). The last two medals are unusual since they were in two different degrees; first class for officers and second class for enlisted personnel.

All foreign medals awarded to members of the U.S. Armed Forces were either furnished by the foreign government or purchased by the recipient since the United States government does not provide foreign medals to members of the Armed Forces.

Designated campaigns for the Vietnam Service Medal

Army and Naval Services:
★ Vietnam (VN) Advisory, 1962 - 1965
★ VN Defense, 1965 - 1965
★ VN Counteroffensive Campaign, 1965 - 1966
★ VN Counteroffensive Campaign Phase II, 1966 -1967
★ VN Counteroffensive Campaign Phase III, 1967 - 1968
★ TET Counteroffensive, 1968
★ VN Counteroffensive Campaign Phase IV, 1968
★ VN Counteroffensive Campaign Phase V, 1968
★ VN Counteroffensive Campaign Phase VI, 1968 - 1969
★ TET69 Counteroffensive, 1969
★ VN Summer - Fall 1969, 1969
★ Vietnam Winter - Spring 1970, 1969 - 1970
★ Sanctuary Counteroffensive, 1970
★ VN Counteroffensive Campaign Phase VII, 1970 - 1971
★ Consolidation I, 1971
★ Consolidation II, 1971 - 1972
★ Vietnam Cease-Fire Campaign, 1972 - 1973

Vietnamese Cross of Gallantry (for valor)

Armed Forces Honor Medal 1st and 2nd class

Civil Actions Medal 1st and 2nd class

Marine Corps' Vietnam Basic Campaign Medals

(Marine Corps Art Collection)

Arrival in Vietnam
When a Marine first arrived in Vietnam and joined his unit, he had already been awarded the National Defense Service Medal and earned a Marksmanship Badge.

A Marine would be authorized the Vietnam Service Medal after 30 days in country and may have already earned 2 campaign stars depending on his arrival date. Depending on the assignment the Marine may have earned the Combat Action Ribbon.

After six months in country this Marine is authorized the South Vietnam Campaign Medal and may have qualified for other awards.

Depending on his lenght of service an enlisted Marine could also have earned the USMC Good Conduct Medal along with the RVN Gallantry Cross Unit Citiation.

Medals of America Press

Marine Corps Order of Precedence and Attachments

The Marine Corps awards system has evolved into a highly structured program often called the "Pyramid of Honor." The system is designed to reward services ranging from heroism on the battlefield to superior performance of non combat duties.

Since World War II the Marine Corps has generally embraced Napoleon's concept of liberally awarding medals and ribbons to enhance morale and esprit de corps. Over the years an expanded and specifically-tailored awards program became generally very popular in the all-volunteer Marine Corps and has played a significant part in improving morale, job performance, recruitment and reenlistments among junior officers and enlisted personnel.

Ribbon Chart Showing All Current Marine Corps Awards

The ribbon chart on the page to the right is provided to diaplay all of the Marine Corps awards from World War II up to today. This is furnished since many Vietnam Marine Corps veterans continued to serve on active duty and in the reserves.

USMC Military Ribbon Chart 1961-1973

This one of a kind ribbon chart on page 32, reads left to right and shows the ribbon for every USMC award during the Vietnam War to include the appropriate devices for each ribbon. Authorized attachments for each ribbon are displayed below the ribbon and a reference bar on the right side of the page provides guides to a detailed device graphic on pages 36-37.

The correct order of precedence for Marine Corps ribbons on page 32 is shown going back to World War II since there were Marine Corps veterans of the Vietnam war who had previously served in World War II and or the Korean War.

The chart does include the Korean Defense Medal which was not authorized during the Vietnam war but was made retro active to 1954, therefore some Marine Corps Vietnam veterans may have also served in Korea during the period of 1961 to 1973 and thus be authorized the award.

USMC Medals and Ribbons Devices

Marine Corps Ribbon Devices (Appurtenances) start on page 34 and examples of Marine Corps ribbon devices are shown correctly mounted to ribbons and medals. For those who desire even more detail charts for proper placement of Marine Corps Ribbon Devices (Appurtenances) are on pages 36-37. All Marine Corps ribbon devices are shown in alphabetical order starting with the Gold Airplane.

Current Marine Corps Ribbons & Devices

Correct Order of Ribbon Wear

The display of new DOD V, C and R devices is based on initial DOD guidance. Their use and application has been announced by the Marine Corps and therefore is the same as shown.

Medal of Honor

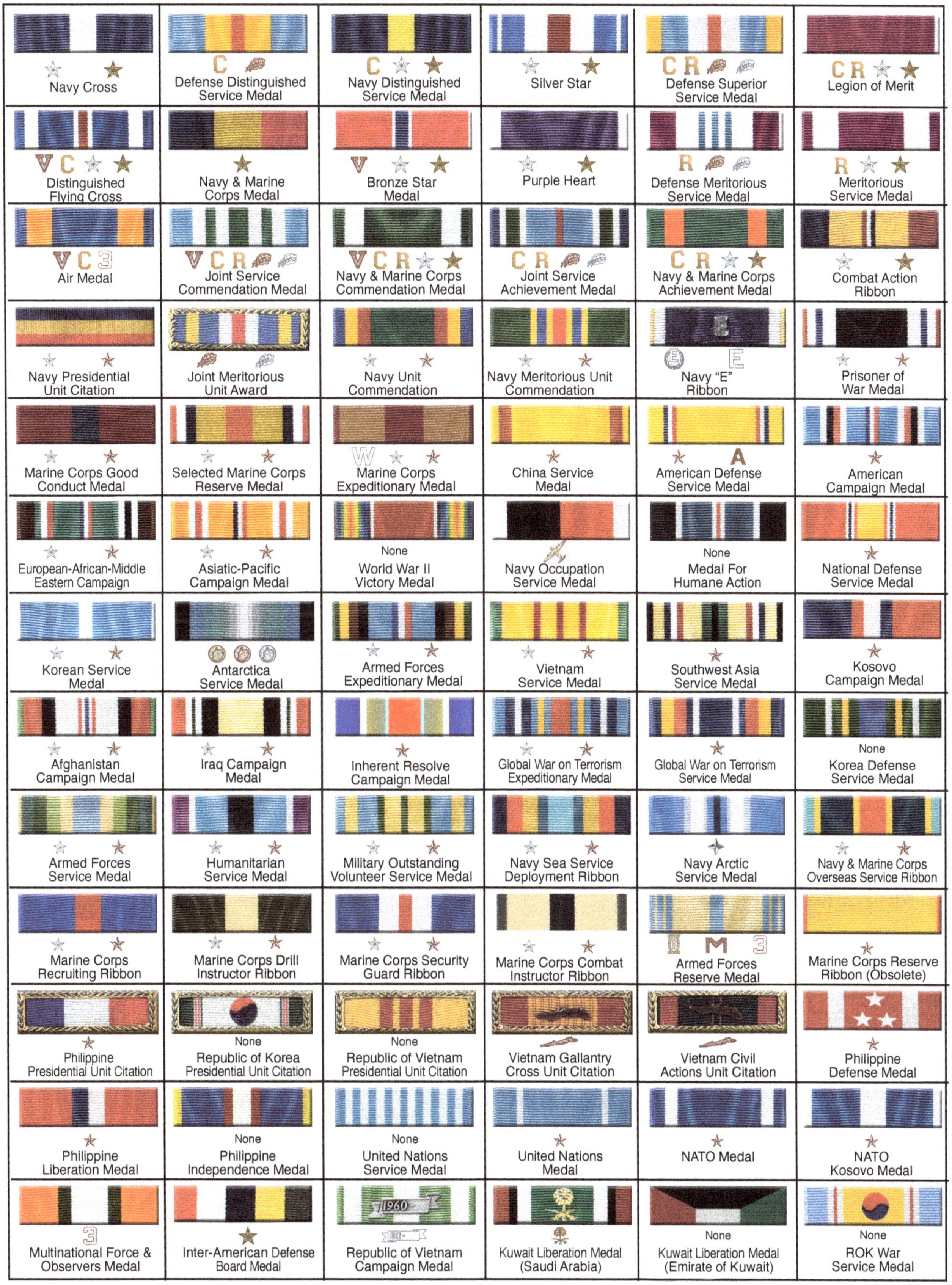

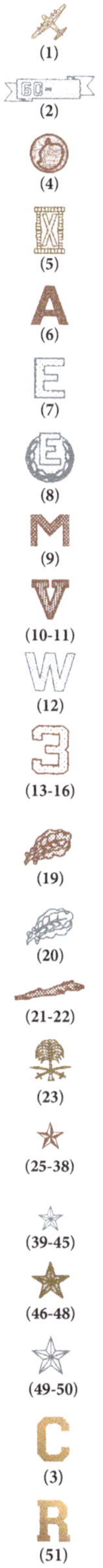

Navy Cross	Defense Distinguished Service Medal	Navy Distinguished Service Medal	Silver Star	Defense Superior Service Medal	Legion of Merit
Distinguished Flying Cross	Navy & Marine Corps Medal	Bronze Star Medal	Purple Heart	Defense Meritorious Service Medal	Meritorious Service Medal
Air Medal	Joint Service Commendation Medal	Navy & Marine Corps Commendation Medal	Joint Service Achievement Medal	Navy & Marine Corps Achievement Medal	Combat Action Ribbon
Navy Presidential Unit Citation	Joint Meritorious Unit Award	Navy Unit Commendation	Navy Meritorious Unit Commendation	Navy "E" Ribbon	Prisoner of War Medal
Marine Corps Good Conduct Medal	Selected Marine Corps Reserve Medal	Marine Corps Expeditionary Medal	China Service Medal	American Defense Service Medal	American Campaign Medal
European-African-Middle Eastern Campaign	Asiatic-Pacific Campaign Medal	World War II Victory Medal	Navy Occupation Service Medal	Medal For Humane Action	National Defense Service Medal
Korean Service Medal	Antarctica Service Medal	Armed Forces Expeditionary Medal	Vietnam Service Medal	Southwest Asia Service Medal	Kosovo Campaign Medal
Afghanistan Campaign Medal	Iraq Campaign Medal	Inherent Resolve Campaign Medal	Global War on Terrorism Expeditionary Medal	Global War on Terrorism Service Medal	Korea Defense Service Medal
Armed Forces Service Medal	Humanitarian Service Medal	Military Outstanding Volunteer Service Medal	Navy Sea Service Deployment Ribbon	Navy Arctic Service Medal	Navy & Marine Corps Overseas Service Ribbon
Marine Corps Recruiting Ribbon	Marine Corps Drill Instructor Ribbon	Marine Corps Security Guard Ribbon	Marine Corps Combat Instructor Ribbon	Armed Forces Reserve Medal	Marine Corps Reserve Ribbon (Obsolete)
Philippine Presidential Unit Citation	Republic of Korea Presidential Unit Citation	Republic of Vietnam Presidential Unit Citation	Vietnam Gallantry Cross Unit Citation	Vietnam Civil Actions Unit Citation	Philippine Defense Medal
Philippine Liberation Medal	Philippine Independence Medal	United Nations Service Medal	United Nations Medal	NATO Medal	NATO Kosovo Medal
Multinational Force & Observers Medal	Inter-American Defense Board Medal	Republic of Vietnam Campaign Medal	Kuwait Liberation Medal (Saudi Arabia)	Kuwait Liberation Medal (Emirate of Kuwait)	ROK War Service Medal

Numbers next to devices provide details on pages 36-37.

Medals of America Press 31

U.S. Marine Corps Ribbons & Devices 1961-1973

Correct Order Of Ribbon Wear During the Vietnam War

Medal of Honor	Navy Cross	Defense Distinguished Service Medal	Navy Distinguished Service Medal	Silver Star	(1)
Legion of Merit	Distinguished Flying Cross	Navy & Marine Corps Medal	Bronze Star Medal	Meritorious Service Medal	(2) (4) (5)
Air Medal	Joint Service Commendation Medal	Navy & Marine Corps Commendation Medal	Navy & Marine Corps Achievement Medal	Purple Heart *Note Below*	(6) (7)
Combat Action Ribbon	Navy Presidential Unit Citation	Navy Unit Commendation	Navy Meritorious Unit Commendation	Navy "E" Ribbon	(8) (9)
Prisoner of War Medal	Marine Corps Good Conduct Medal	Selected Marine Corps Reserve Medal	Marine Corps Expeditionary Medal	China Service Medal	(10-11) (12)
American Defense Service Medal	American Campaign Medal	European-African-Middle Eastern Campaign	Asiatic-Pacific Campaign Medal	None — World War II Victory Medal	(13-16) (19)
Navy Occupation Service Medal	None — Medal For Humane Action	National Defense Service Medal	Korean Service Medal	Antarctica Service Medal	(20) (21-22)
Armed Forces Expeditionary Medal	Vietnam Service Medal	None — Korea Defense Service Medal	Armed Forces Reserve Medal	Marine Corps Reserve Ribbon (Obsolete)	(23) (25-38)
Foreign Decoration	Philippine Presidential Unit Citation	None — Republic of Korea Presidential Unit Citation	None — Republic of Vietnam Presidential Unit Citation	Vietnam Gallantry Cross Unit Citation	(39-45) (46-48)
Vietnam Civil Actions Unit Citation	Philippine Defense Medal	Philippine Liberation Medal	None — Philippine Independence Medal	None — United Nations Service Medal	(49-50)
United Nations Medal	Multinational Force & Observers Medal	Inter-American Defense Board Medal	Republic of Vietnam Campaign Medal	None — ROK War Service Medal	Numbers next to devices provide details on pages 36-37.

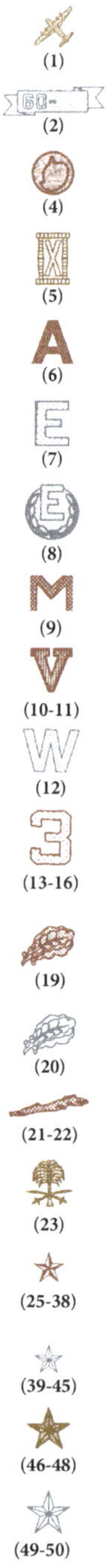

Note: Per Marine Corps regulations, no row may contain more than four (4) ribbons. The above display is arranged solely to conserve space on the page. *The Purple Heart Medal was moved behind the Bronze Star Medal in 1985.*

32 **Marine Corps Medals, Badges & Insignia Vietnam**

Placement of Breast Insignia, Ribbons and Badges

Wearing ribbons and badges of the United States Marine Corps

Service Ribbons - Ribbons are normally worn in rows of three or four if you are displaying a large number of awards. If your coat lapel conceals any ribbons they may be placed in successively decreasing rows ie: (4,3,2,1). All aligned vertically on the center, except the top row can be altered to present the neatest appearance. You can space your ribbon rows 1/8 inch apart or together (See both examples on this page). When marksmanship badges are worn, the ribbon bars are 1/8 inch above them. You wear all ribbons to which entitled on your service and dress "B" coats. Ribbon only awards are worn on the dress "A" coats above the upper right pocket when full size medals are worn over the upper left pocket.

The first row of ribbons will be 1/8 of an inch above the top edge of the shooting badges. The second and succeeding rows of ribbons will either be worn 1/8 of an inch apart or flush. Flush example above.

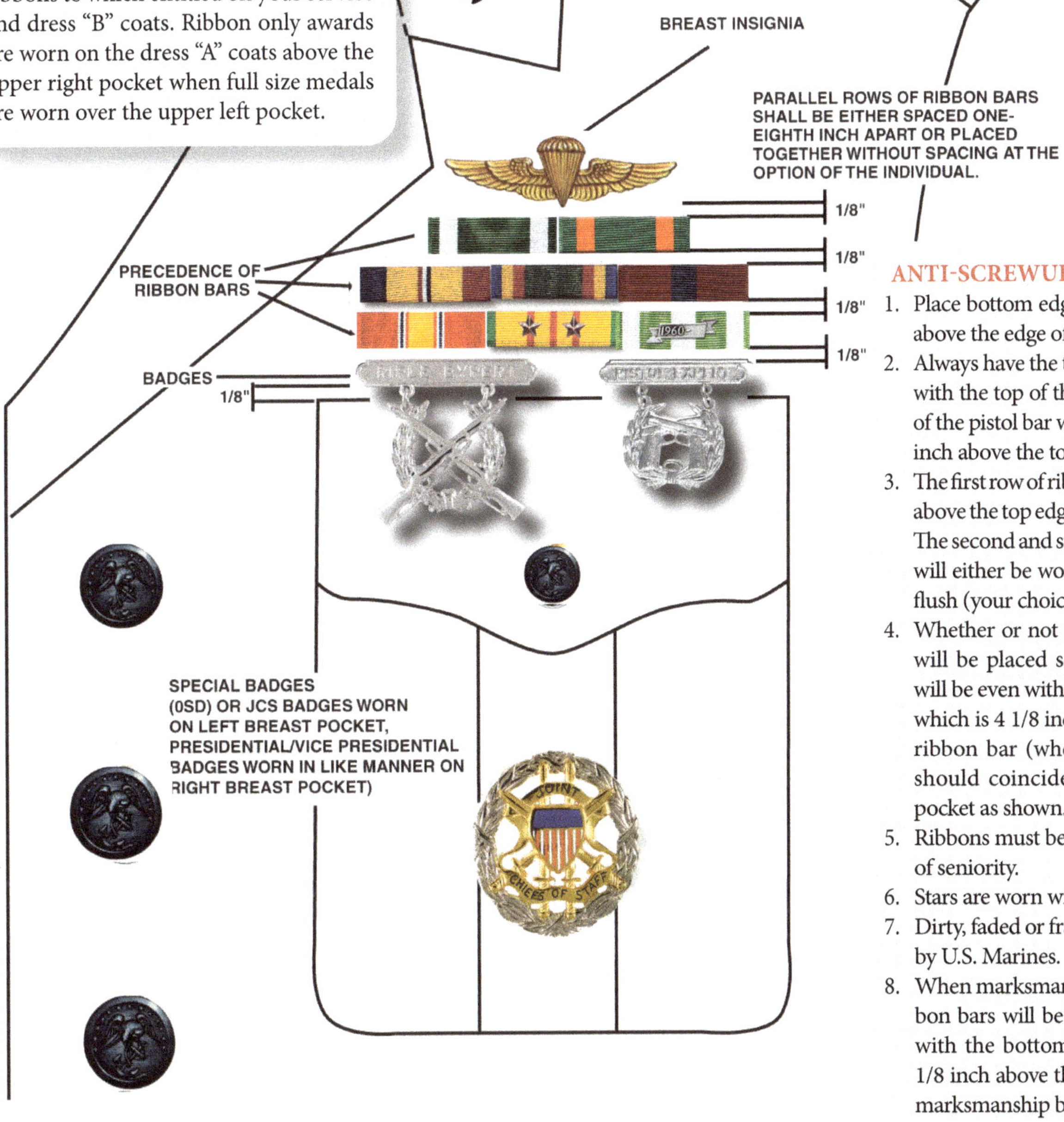

BREAST INSIGNIA

PARALLEL ROWS OF RIBBON BARS SHALL BE EITHER SPACED ONE-EIGHTH INCH APART OR PLACED TOGETHER WITHOUT SPACING AT THE OPTION OF THE INDIVIDUAL.

PRECEDENCE OF RIBBON BARS

1/8"
1/8"
1/8"
1/8"

BADGES
1/8"

SPECIAL BADGES (OSD) OR JCS BADGES WORN ON LEFT BREAST POCKET, PRESIDENTIAL/VICE PRESIDENTIAL BADGES WORN IN LIKE MANNER ON RIGHT BREAST POCKET)

ANTI-SCREWUP WEAR GUIDANCE:

1. Place bottom edge of the rifle bar 1/8 inch above the edge of your pocket.
2. Always have the top of your pistol bar even with the top of the rifle bar; so the bottom of the pistol bar will be more than 1/8 of an inch above the top edge of the pocket.
3. The first row of ribbons will be 1/8 of an inch above the top edge of your shooting badges. The second and succeeding rows of ribbons will either be worn 1/8 of an inch apart or flush (your choice!).
4. Whether or not ribbons are worn, badges will be placed so that the outboard end will be even with the end of the ribbon bar, which is 4 1/8 inch long. The center of this ribbon bar (whether real or imaginary) should coincide with the center of the pocket as shown.
5. Ribbons must be worn in the proper order of seniority.
6. Stars are worn with one point right up.
7. Dirty, faded or frayed ribbons are not worn by U.S. Marines.
8. When marksmanship badge is a worn, ribbon bars will be centered over the pocket with the bottom edge of the ribbon bar 1/8 inch above the widest holding bar of a marksmanship badge(s).

Medals of America Press 33

Placement of Devices on Ribbons

No. of Awards	3/16 Bronze and Silver Campaign Stars	Letter V*	Air Medal Individual	Air Medal Strike Flight
1				
2				
3				
4				
5				
6				
7				
8				
9				
10				

Air Medal (1980-1989, 2006-Current)

 Bronze Block Numerals

Gold Block Numerals

Air Medal (1989-2006)

Armed Forces Reserve Medal

After 10 years of reserve service

With 1 mobilization

With 2 mobilizations

After 10 years of reserve service and 3 mobilizations

Legend:

 = Bronze Letter "M"

 = Hourglass

 = Letter "V"

 = 5/16" dia. Gold Star

 = 5/16" dia. Silver Star

 = Bronze or Gold Block Numerals

 = Bronze or Silver Oak Leaf Cluster

 = 3/16" dia. Bronze Star

 = 3/16" dia. Silver Star

Placement of Devices on Ribbons

Placement of Oak Leaf Cluster Devices on the Ribbon

No. of Awards	USMC	No. of Awards	USMC
1		6	
2		7	
3		8	
4		9	
5		10	SEE NOTE 1

USMC

Same as ribbons to the left but placed vertically

NOTE: 1

1. DOD Regulations limit the number of Oak Leafs which may be worn on a single ribbon to a maximum of four (4). If more than four devices are authorized, a second ribbon is worn containing the excess devices.

Legend:
- ★ = ⁵⁄₁₆" **Bronze Star**
- ★ = ⁵⁄₁₆" **Silver Star**
- = Bronze Oak Leaf Cluster
- = Silver Oak Leaf Cluster

Medals of America Press 35

U.S. Marine Corps Ribbons Devices

1. Airplane, C-54, Gold

Services: All
Worn on: World War II Occupation Medals
Denotes: Service during Berlin Airlift (1948-49)

2. Bar, Date, Silver

Services: All
Worn on: Republic of Vietnam Campaign Medal
Denotes: Worn upon initial issue; has no significance

3. Letter "C", Serif, Gold

Services: All
Worn on: Personal Decorations
Denotes: Award earned in a combat setting.

4a. Disk, Bronze, Gold, Silver

Worn on: Antarctica Service Medal
Denotes: Wintered over 1,2 or 3 times on the Antarctic continent

5a. Hourglass, Bronze

Services: All
Worn on: Armed Forces Reserve Medal
Denotes: 10 Years of service in the Reserve Forces

5b. Hourglass, Silver

Services: All
Worn on: Armed Forces Reserve Medal
Denotes: 20 Years of service in the Reserve Forces

5c. Hourglass, Gold

Services: All
Worn on: Armed Forces Reserve Medal
Denotes: 30 Years of service in the Reserve Forces

6. Letter "A", Block, Bronze

Services: Navy, Marine Corps, Coast Guard
Worn on: American Defense Service Medal
Denotes: Atlantic Fleet service prior to World War II

7. Letter "E", Block, Silver

Services: Navy, Marine Corps.
Worn on: Navy "E" Ribbon
Denotes: Initial and subsequent awards (3 maximum)

8. Letter "E", Wreathed, Silver

Services: Navy, Marine Corps.
Worn on: Navy "E" Ribbon
Denotes: Fourth (Final) award

9. Letter "M", Block, Bronze

Services: All
Worn on: Armed Forces Reserve Medal
Denotes: Mobilization for active military service

10. Letter "V", Serif, Bronze

Services: All
Worn on: Joint Service Commendation Medal
Denotes: Valorous actions in combat

11. Letter "V", Serif, Gold

Services: Marine Corps
Worn on: Personal Decorations
Denotes: Valorous actions in combat

12. Letter "W", Block, Silver

Services: Navy, Marine Corps.
Worn on: Expeditionary Medals
Denotes: Participation in the defense of Wake Island (Dec, 1941)

13. Numeral, Block, Bronze

Services: Navy, Marine Corps.
Worn on: Air Medal
Denotes: Total number of Strike/Flight awards

14. Numeral, Block, Bronze

Services: All (Except Coast Guard)
Worn on: Humanitarian Service Medal
Denotes: Number of additional awards (Obsolete)

15. Numeral, Block, Bronze

Services: All
Worn on: Armed Forces Reserve Medal
Denotes: Number of times mobilized for active duty

16. Numeral, Block, Bronze

Services: All
Worn on: Multinational Force & Observers Medal
Denotes: Total number of awards

17. Numeral, Block, Gold

Services: Navy, Marine Corps
Worn on: Air Medal
Denotes: Total number of individual awards

18. Numeral, Scroll, Bronze

Services: Marine Corps
Worn on: Marine Corps Good Conduct and Expeditionary Medals
Denotes: Number of awards (Obsolete)

19. Oak Leaf Cluster, Bronze

Services: All
Worn on: Joint Service Decorations and Joint Meritorious Unit Award
Denotes: One (1) additional award

20. Oak Leaf Cluster, Silver

Services: All
Worn on: Joint Service decorations and Joint Meritorious Unit Award
Denotes: Five (5) additional awards

21. Palm, Bronze

Services: All (Except Army)
Worn on: Vietnam Gallantry Cross Unit Citation
Denotes: No significance, worn upon initial issue

22. Palm, Bronze

Services: All
Worn on: Vietnam Civil Actions Unit Citation
Denotes: No significance, worn upon initial issue

23. Palm & Swords Device, Gold

Services: All
Worn on: Kuwait Liberation Medal (Saudi Arabia)
Denotes: No significance, worn upon initial issue

24. Star 3/16" dia., Blue

Services: Navy, Marine Corps
Worn on: Navy Presidential Unit Citation
Denotes: Initial and subsequent awards (Obsolete)

25. Star 3/16" dia., Bronze

Services: All
Worn on: Campaign awards since World War II
Denotes: Battle participation (one star per major engagement)

26. Star 3/16" dia., Bronze

Services: All
Worn on: Expeditionary Medals
Denotes: Additional service (one star per designated expedition)

27. Star 3/16" dia., Bronze

Services: All
Worn on: Prisoner of War and Humanitarian Service Medals
Denotes: One (1) additional award

28. Star 3/16" dia., Bronze

Services: Navy, Marine Corps.
Worn on: Unit Awards
Denotes: One (1) star per each additional award

29. Star 3/16" dia., Bronze

Services: All
Worn on: Service Awards
Denotes: One (1) star per each additional award

30. Star 3/16" dia., Bronze

Services: Navy and Marine Corps.
Worn on: Air Medal
Denotes: First individual award (Obsolete)

31. Star 3/16" dia., Bronze

Services: All
Worn on: World War I Victory Medal
Denotes: One (1) star for each campaign clasp earned

32. Star 3/16" dia., Bronze

Services: Navy, Marine Corps, Coast Guard
Worn on: China Service Medal (1937-39)
Denotes: Additional award for service during (1945-57)

33. Star 3/16" dia., Bronze

Services: All
Worn on: American Defense Service Medal
Denotes: Overseas service prior to World War II

36. Star 3/16" dia., Bronze

Services: All
Worn on: National Defense Service Medal
Denotes: Additional awards (one star per designated period)

37. Star 3/16" dia., Bronze

Services: All
Worn on: Philippine Defense and Liberation Ribbons
Denotes: Additional battle honors

38. Star 3/16" dia., Bronze

Services: All (Except Army)
Worn on: Philippine Presidential Unit Citation
Denotes: Additional award

39. Star 3/16" dia., Bronze

Services: All
Worn on: United Nations and NATO mission medals
Denotes: One (1) star for each additional mission

40. Star 3/16" dia., Silver

Services: All
Worn on: Campaign awards since World War II
Denotes: Battle participation in five (5) major engagements

41. Star 3/16" dia., Silver

Services: All
Worn on: Expeditionary Medals
Denotes: Five (5) additional expeditions

42. Star 3/16" dia., Silver

Services: All
Worn on: Prisoner of War and Humanitarian Service Medals
Denotes: Five (5) additional awards

43. Star 3/16" dia., Silver

Services: Navy, Marine Corps
Worn on: Unit awards
Denotes: Five (5) additional awards

44. Star 3/16" dia., Silver

Services: All
Worn on: Service Awards
Denotes: Five (5) additional Awards

45. Star 5/16" dia., Bronze

Services: Navy, Marine Corps.
Worn on: Navy, USMC Expeditionary Medals
Denotes: One (1) additional award (Obsolete)

45. Star 5/16" dia., Bronze

Services: Navy, Marine Corps.
Worn on: Haitian Campaign Medal (1915)
Denotes: Subsequent award of the "1919-1920" Clasp

46. Star 5/16" dia., Gold

Services: Navy, Marine Corps, Coast Guard
Worn on: Personal Decorations
Denotes: One (1) additional award

47. Star 5/16" dia., Gold

Services: Navy, Marine Corps
Worn on: Combat Action Ribbon
Denotes: One (1) additional award

48. Star 5/16" dia., Gold

Services: All
Worn on: Inter-American Defense Board Medal
Denotes: One (1) additional award

49. Star 5/16" dia., Silver

Services: Navy, Marine Corps
Worn on: Combat Action Ribbon
Denotes: Five (5) additional award

50. Star 5/16" dia., Silver

Services: Navy, Marine Corps, Coast Guard
Worn on: Personal Decorations
Denotes: Five (5) additional awards

51. Star 5/16" dia., Silver

Services: Navy
Worn on: World War II Campaign Medals
Denotes: Five (5) major campaigns (Obsolete)

52. Letter "R", serif, Bronze

Services: All
Worn on: Personal Decorations
Denotes: Recognizes remote combat action

53. North Star

Services: Navy, Marine
Worn on: Artic Circle Medal
Denotes: Up to 4 awards

V,C and R Devices as proposed by DOD in 2016
Their use is approved by the USMC Awards Board.

VCR

The Department of Defense conducted a year-long review of the military decorations and awards program to ensure appropriate recognition of the service, sacrifices, and actions of service members while maintaining the historical legacy of the awards program. The department's review focused on combat and valor recognition utilizing lessons learned over 14 years of combat operations. Among the key changes are:

- Standardization of the meaning and use of the "V" device as a valor-only device to ensure unambiguous and distinctive recognition for preeminent acts of combat valor;
- Creation of a new combat device (e.g., "C" device) to distinctly recognize those service members performing meritoriously under the most arduous combat conditions;
- Introduction of an "R" remote impacts device to recognize service members who use remote technology to directly impact combat operations.

These changes are retroactive to Jan. 2016 and will result in different guidelines for devices for each branch (Army, Navy etc.) based on service before 2016 and service after 2016. Past awards of the V device before 2016 remain valid.

Right Breast Displays on Full Dress Uniforms

When large medals are worn, all unit citations and ribbons with no medals authorized are centered over the right breast pocket the bottom edge 1/8 inch above the top of the pocket. Note pre 1985 placement of Purple Heart Medal.

(**Marine Corps Art Collection**)

The Marine Corps prescribe the wear of "ribbon only" awards on the right breast of the full dress uniform when large medals are worn. The current required Marine Corps displays is shown below and contains all the *Ribbon Only* awards issued before, during and after the Vietnam War for Marine Corps veterans with continued service after the Vietnam War.

Shown when Philippine Awards were Ribbons

	Combat Action Ribbon	
Navy Presidential Unit Citation	Joint Meritorious Unit Award	Navy Unit Commendation
Navy Meritorious Unit Commendation	Navy "E" Ribbon	Sea Service Deployment Ribbon
Arctic Service Ribbon	Navy & Marine Corps Overseas Svs Ribbon	Marine Corps Recruiting Ribbon
Marine Corps Drill Instructor Ribbon	Marine Corps Security Guard Ribbon	Marine Corps Combat Instructor Ribbon
Marine Corps Reserve Ribbon	Philippine Presidential Unit Citation	Korean Presidential Unit Citation
Vietnam Presidential Unit Citation	Vietnam Gallantry Cross Unit Citation	Vietnam Civil Actions Unit Citation
Philippine Defense Ribbon	Philippine Liberation Ribbon	Philippine Independence Ribbon

38 Marine Corps Medals, Badges & Insignia Vietnam

Veterans Wearing Medals

Introduction

One of the first lessons taught to new Marines is proper wear of the uniform and insignia. The same rules apply to veterans and retirees wearing military awards on their former uniform or civilian dress. There are many occasions today when tradition, patriotism, ceremonies and social occasions call for the wear of military awards.

Civilian Dress

The most common manner of wearing a decoration or medal is as a lapel pin in the left lapel of a civilian suit jacket. The small enameled lapel pin represents a decoration or medal an individual has received (usually the highest award or one having special meaning to the wearer). Many veterans always wear a lapel pin. Lapel pins are available for all awards and ribbons.

Honorably discharged and retired Marines members may wear full-size or miniature medals on civilian suits for appropriate occasions such as Memorial Day and Armed Forces Day. Female members may wear full-size or miniature medals on equivalent dress. It is not considered appropriate to wear skill or qualification badges on civilian attire.

Formal Civilian Wear

For more formal occasions, it is correct and encouraged to wear miniature decorations and medals. For a black or white tie occasion, the rule is quite simple: if the lapel is wide enough wear the miniatures on the left lapel or, in the case of a shawl lapel on a tuxedo, the miniature medals are worn over the left breast pocket. The center of the holding bar of the bottom row of medals should be parallel to the ground immediately above the pocket. Do not wear a pocket handkerchief.

Wear of the Uniform

On certain occasions, retired Marine personnel may wear either the uniform prescribed at the date of retirement or any of the current active duty authorized uniforms. Retirees should adhere to the same grooming standards as Marine active duty personnel when wearing the uniform (for example, a beard is inappropriate while in uniform). Whenever the uniform is worn, it must be done in such a manner as to reflect credit upon the individual and the Marine Corps. (Do not mix uniform items.)

The occasions for uniform wear by retirees are
Military ceremonies, funerals, weddings, memorial services and inaugurals.
Patriotic parades on national holidays.
Military parades in which active or reserve units are participating.
Educational institutions when engaged in giving military instruction. Social or other functions when the invitation has obviously been influenced by the member's earlier active service.

Honorably separated wartime veterans may wear the uniform authorized at the time of their service for:
Military funerals, memorial services, and inaugurals.
Patriotic parades on national holidays.
Military parades in which active or reserve units are participating.

Non-wartime Marine personnel separated (other than retired and Reserve) are not authorized to wear the uniform but may wear the medals.

Introduction to U.S. Marine Corps Medals

Beginning with the Navy, Marine Corps and Coast Guard Medal of Honor the decorations, medals and ribbon awards of the United States Marine Corps are presented in their order of precedence from 1961 to 1973.

THE MEDAL OF HONOR

In a country whose government is based upon a totally democratic society, it is fitting that the first medal to reward meritorious acts on the field of battle should be for private soldiers, marines, and seamen (although later extended to officers).

The Congressional Medal of Honor (referred to universally as the Medal of Honor in all statutes, awards manuals and uniform regulations) was born in conflict and steeped in controversy during its early years, finally emerging, along with Great Britain's Victoria Cross, as one of the World's premier awards for bravery.

The Medal of Honor comes in three forms (Army, Navy and Air Force); all three medals represent our county's highest reward for bravery. Today there is only one set of directives governing the award of this, the highest of all U.S. decorations.

The medal was created during the Civil War as a reward for "gallantry in action and other soldier-like qualities." However, the reference to "other qualities" led to many awards for actions which would seem less than heroic, including the bestowal of 864 awards upon the entire membership of the 27th Maine Volunteer Infantry for merely reenlisting.

The inconsistencies in this and other dubious cases were apparently resolved in the early 20th Century when 910 names were removed from the lists (including the 864 awarded to the 27th Maine). At the same time, the statutes which intrepidity govern the award of the medal were revised to reflect the present-day criteria of "gallantry and at the risk of one's own life above and beyond the call of duty."

A listing of all Marine Corps recipients of the Medal of Honor maybe found on WWW. Homeofheroes.com.

MEDAL OF HONOR
(Navy-Marine Corps-Coast Guard Design)

Navy Medal of Honor (Current)

THE NAVY MEDAL OF HONOR

"For conspicuous gallantry and intrepidity at the risk of life, above and beyond the call of duty, in action, involving actual conflict with an opposing armed force." The Medal of Honor is worn before all other decorations and medals and is the highest honor that can be conferred on a member of the Armed Forces. Since its inception, 3,432 Medal of Honor have been awarded to 3,408 individuals, 249 to Marines.

Many Americans today are confused with the term "Congressional Medal of Honor," when, in fact, the proper term is "Medal of Honor.". Part of this confusion stems from the fact that all MOH recipients belong to the Congressional Medal of Honor Society chartered by Congress.

An act of Congress in July 1963 clarified and amended the criteria for awarding the Medal of Honor to prevent award of the medal for deeds done "in line of profession," but not necessarily in actual conflict with an enemy. This act of Congress made the clarification by stating that the award was "for service in military operations involving conflict with an opposing force or for such service with friendly forces engaged in armed conflict."

A recommendation for the Navy Medal of Honor must be made within three years from the date of the deed upon which it depends and award of the medal must be made within five years after the date of the deed. A stipulation for the medal is that there must be a minimum of two witnesses to the deed, who swear separately that the event transpired as stated in the final citation.

The Navy Medal of Honor is a five pointed star with a standing figure of the Goddess Minerva surrounded by a circle of stars representing the number of States in the Union at the outbreak of the Civil War. Minerva, the Goddess of Strength and Wisdom, holds a shield taken from the Great Seal of the United States, and in her left hand she holds a fasces, which represents the lawful authority of the state; she is warding off a crouching figure representing Discord. The medal is suspended from an anchor and the reverse is plain for engraving the recipient's name. The ribbon is light blue and has an eight-sided central pad with thirteen white stars.

Navy Cross

Instituted: 1919

Criteria: Extraordinary heroism in action against an enemy of the U.S. while engaged in military operations involving conflict with an opposing foreign force or while serving with friendly foreign forces

Devices:

Notes: Originally issued with a 1 1/2" wide ribbon

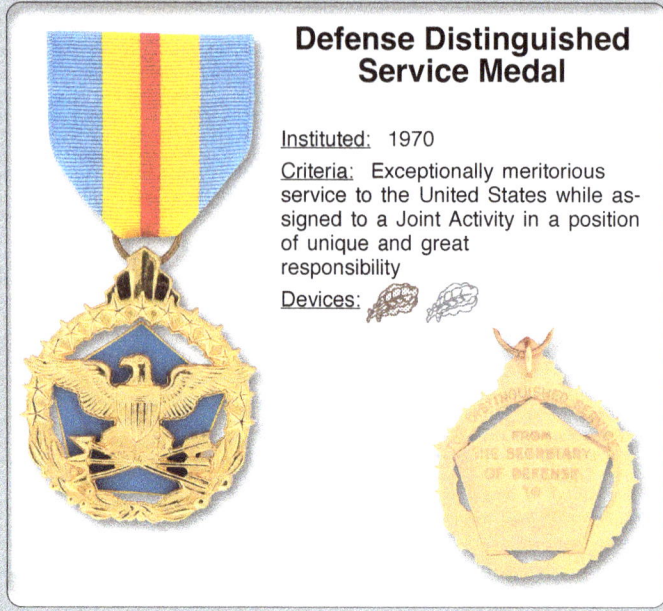

Defense Distinguished Service Medal

Instituted: 1970

Criteria: Exceptionally meritorious service to the United States while assigned to a Joint Activity in a position of unique and great responsibility

Devices:

Navy Distinguished Service Medal

Instituted: 1919

Criteria: Exceptionally meritorious service to the U.S. Government in a duty of great responsibility

Devices:

Silver Star

Instituted: 1932

Criteria: Gallantry in action against an armed enemy of the United States or while serving with friendly foreign forces

Devices:

Notes: Derived from the 3/16" silver "Citation Star" previously worn on Army campaign medals

Legion of Merit

Instituted: 1942

Criteria: Exceptionally meritorious conduct in the performance of outstanding services to the United States

Devices:

Notes: Issued in four degrees (Legionnaire, Officer, Commander & Chief Commander) to foreign nationals

Distinguished Flying Cross

Instituted: 1926

Criteria: Heroism or extraordinary achievement while participating in aerial flight

Devices:

42 Marine Corps Medals, Badges & Insignia Vietnam

Navy and Marine Corps Medal

Instituted: 1942

Criteria: Heroism not involving actual conflict with an armed enemy of the United States

Devices:

Notes: For acts of lifesaving, action must be at great risk to one's own life.

Bronze Star Medal

Instituted: 1944

Criteria: Heroic or meritorious achievement or service not involving participation in aerial flight

Devices:

Purple Heart

Instituted: 1932

Criteria: Awarded to any member of the U.S. Armed Forces killed or wounded in an armed conflict

Devices:

Prior to 1985 the Purple Heart Medal was ranked just before the Combat Action Ribbon as shown on the Vietnam Era Ribbon Chart. This is today's location.

Meritorious Service Medal

Instituted: 1969

Criteria: Outstanding **noncombat** meritorious achievement or service to the United States

Devices:

Air Medal

Instituted: 1942

Criteria: Heroic actions or meritorious service while participating in aerial flight

Devices:

Joint Service Commendation Medal

Instituted: 1963

Criteria: Meritorious service or achievement while assigned to a Joint Activity

Devices: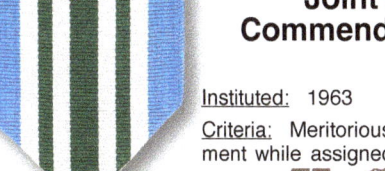

Medals of America Press

Navy & Marine Corps Commendation Medal

Instituted: 1950

Criteria: Meritorious service or achievement in a combat or noncombat situation based on sustained performance of a superlative nature

Devices:

Notes: Originally a ribbon-only award then designated "Navy Commendation Ribbon with Metal Pendant". Redesignated: "Navy Commendation Medal" in 1960. Change to present name was made in 1994.

Navy & Marine Corps Achievement Medal

Instituted: 1961

Criteria: Meritorious service or achievement in a combat or noncombat situation based on sustained performance of a superlative nature

Devices:

Notes: Originally a ribbon-only award: "Secretary of the Navy Commendation for Achievement Award with Ribbon". Changed to present form in 1967. Changed to present name in 1994.

Combat Action Ribbon

Instituted: 1969   Devices:

Criteria: Active participation in ground or air combat during specifically listed military operations

Notes: This is the only Navy personal decoration which has no associated medal (a "ribbon-only" award)

Navy Presidential Unit Citation

Instituted: 1942   Devices:

Criteria: Awarded to Navy/Marine Corps units for extraordinary heroism in action against an armed enemy

Navy Unit Commendation

Instituted: 1944   Devices:

Criteria: Awarded to units Navy/Marine Corps for outstanding heroism in action or extremely meritorious service

Navy Meritorious Unit Commendation Ribbon

Instituted: 1967   Devices:

Criteria: Awarded to Navy/Marine Corps units for valorous actions or meritorious achievement (combat or noncombat)

Navy "E" Ribbon

Instituted: 1976   Devices:

Criteria: Awarded to ships or squadrons which have won battle efficiency competitions

Prisoner of War Medal

Instituted: 1985, retroactive to 5 April 1917

Criteria: Awarded to any member of the U.S. Armed Forces taken prisoner during any armed conflict dating from World War I

Devices:

Marine Corps Good Conduct Medal

Service: Marine Corps

Instituted: 1896

Criteria: Outstanding performance and conduct during 3 years of continuous active enlisted service in the U.S. Marine Corps

Devices:

Selected Marine Corps Reserve Medal

Service: Marine Corps
Instituted: 1939
Criteria: Outstanding performance and conduct during 4 years service in the Marine Corps Selected Reserve
Devices: ★ ☆

Notes: Formerly: "Organized Marine Corps Reserve Medal".

Marine Corps Expeditionary Medal

Service: Marine Corps
Instituted: 1919
Dates: 1919 to Present
Criteria: Landings on foreign territory and operations against armed opposition for which no specific campaign medal has been authorized
Devices:
Bars: "Wake Island"

China Service Medal

Instituted: 1940
Dates: 1937-39, 1945-57
Criteria: Service ashore in china or on-board naval vessels during either of the above periods
Devices: ★

Notes: Medal was reinstituted in 1947 for extended service during dates shown above.

American Defense Service Medal

Instituted: 1941
Dates: 1939-41
Criteria: For active duty during national and limited emergencies just prior to World War II
Devices:  Bars: "Base", "Fleet"

American Campaign Medal

Instituted: 1942
Dates: 1941-46
Criteria: Service outside the U.S. in the American theater for 30 days, or within the continental U.S. for one year
Devices: ★

European-African-Middle Eastern Campaign Medal

Instituted: 1942
Dates: 1941-45
Criteria: Service in the European-African-Middle Eastern theater for 30 days or receipt of any combat decoration
Devices: ★ ☆

Medals of America Press

Asiatic-Pacific Campaign Medal

Instituted: 1942

Dates: 1941-46

Criteria: Service in the Asiatic-Pacific theater for 30 day or receipt of any combat decoration

Devices:

World War II Victory Medal

Instituted: 1945

Dates: 1941-46

Criteria: Awarded for service in the U.S. Armed Forces during the above period

Devices: None

Navy Occupation Service Medal

Instituted: 1948

Dates: 1945-55 (Berlin: 1945-90)

Criteria: 30 consecutive days of service in occupied territories of former enemies during above period

Devices:

Bars: "Europe," "Asia"

Medal for Humane Action

Instituted: 1949

Dates: 1948-49

Criteria: 120 consecutive days of service participating in the Berlin Airlift or in support thereof

Devices: None

Notes: This medal was only awarded for Berlin Airlift service and is not to be confused with the Humanitarian Service Medal (established in 1977)

National Defense Service Medal

Instituted: 1953

Dates: 1950-54, 1961-74, 1990-95, 11 Sept 2001 - Dec 2022

Criteria: Any honorable active duty service during any of the above periods

Devices:

Korean Service Medal

Instituted: 1950

Dates: 1950-54

Criteria: Participation in military operations within the Korean area during the above period

Devices:

46 Marine Corps Medals, Badges & Insignia Vietnam

Antarctica Service Medal

Instituted: 1960

Dates: 1946 - Present

Criteria: 30 calendar days of service on the Antarctic Continent

Devices:

Bars: "Wintered Over" in bronze, gold, silver

Armed Forces Expeditionary Medal

Instituted: 1961

Dates: 1958 to Present

Criteria: Participation in military operations not covered by a specific campaign medal

Devices:

Notes: Authorized for service in Vietnam until establishment of Vietnam Service Medal.

Vietnam Service Medal

Instituted: 1965

Dates: 1965-73

Criteria: Service in Vietnam, Laos, Cambodia or Thailand during the above period

Devices:

Armed Forces Reserve Medal

Instituted: 1950

Dates: 1949 - Present

Criteria: 10 years of honorable service in any reserve component of the United States Armed Forces

Devices:

Marine Corps Reserve Ribbon

Instituted: 1945

Dates: 1945-1965

Criteria: Successful completion of 10 years of honorable service in any class of the Marine Corps Reserve

Devices:

Korean Defense Service Medal

Instituted: 2003

Dates: 1954- to date TBD

Criteria: For service in the Republic of Korea, or waters adjacent thereto, for a qualifying period of time between 28 July, 1954 and a date to be determine.

Devices: None

Medals of America Press

⭐ Award of Foreign Military Decorations

Authorized foreign decorations for wear by United States Armed Forces are military decorations *(as opposed to service medals)* which have been approved for wear by the Department of Defense but whose awarding authority is a foreign government. French British, Italian and other Allies decorations were presented to U.S. service members extensively during World War I and World War II. In World War I and II the French and Beligium Croix de Guerre were the most commonly awarded decorations to United States service members of all ranks.

Republic of Vietnam military awards *(South Vietnam decorations)* were first awarded to United States service members beginning around 1964. The Vietnamese Gallantry Cross and the Vietnamese Civil Actions Medal were awarded to many U.S. servicemen for heroism and meritorious service.

Foreign campaign *(service)* medals and unit awards have also been awarded U.S. military personnel. Those that were commonly awarded to U.S. military personnel are covered in the following pages.

While each service has its own order of precedence, these general rules typically apply to all services when wearing foreign awards:

U.S. military personal decorations
U.S. military unit awards
U.S. non-military personal decorations (in order of receipt; if from the same service)
U.S. non-military unit awards
U.S. military campaign and service medals
U.S. military service and training awards (ribbon-only awards)
U.S. Merchant Marine awards and non-military service awards
Foreign military personal decorations
Foreign military unit awards
International decorations & service medals (United Nations, NATO, etc.)
Foreign military service awards
Marksmanship awards (Air Force, Navy & Coast Guard)
State awards of the National Guard (Army & Air Force only)

⭐ South Vietnamese Decorations Generally Awarded

Republic of Vietnam Gallantry Cross
Country: Republic of Vietnam
Instituted: 1950
Criteria: Deeds of valor and acts of courage/heroism while fighting the enemy.
Devices:

- Army Level
- Corps Level
- Division Level
- Regt. Level

Republic of Vietnam Armed Forces Honor Medal
Country: Republic of Vietnam
Instituted: 1953
Criteria: For outstanding contributions to the training and development of RVN Armed Forces.
Devices: None
Notes: *1st Class for officers is shown; the 2nd Class medal is in silver and ribbon does not have the yellow edge stripes.*

Republic of Vietnam Staff Service Medal
Country: Republic of Vietnam
Instituted: 1964
Criteria: Awarded for staff service to the Armed Forces evidencing outstanding initiative and devotion to duty.
Notes: *Occasionally called Staff Service Honor Medal. 1st Class has green edge, 2nd Class for enlisted has blue ribbon edge.*

First Class

Second Class

Republic of Vietnam Technical Service Medal
Country: Republic of Vietnam
Instituted: 1964
Criteria: Awarded to military servicemen and civilians working as military technicians who have shown outstanding professional capacity, initiative, and devotion to duty.
Notes: *Second Class medal ribbon awarded to NCOs and enlisted men does not have 2 center red stripes. Occasionally called Technical Services Honor Medal.*

First Class

Republic of Vietnam Training Medal

Country: Republic of Vietnam
Instituted: 1964
Criteria: Awarded to instructors and cadres at military schools and training centers and civilians and foreigners who contribute significantly to training.

Notes: 1st Class Medal is awarded to officers and is occasionally referred to as the Training Service Honor Medal. 2nd Class medal ribbon awarded to NCOs and enlisted men does not have 2 center pink stripes.

First Class

Republic of Vietnam Civil Actions Medal

Country: Republic of Vietnam
Instituted: 1964
Criteria: For outstanding achievements in the field of civic actions.
Devices: None

Notes: *1st Class for officers is shown; the 2nd Class ribbon has no center red stripes. Also awarded as a unit award. Sometimes called Civic Actions Honor Medal.*

Republic of Vietnam Gallantry Cross Unit Citation

Instituted: 1966
Criteria: Awarded to certain units of the U.S. Armed Forces for valorous combat achievement during the Vietnam War, 1 March 1961 to 28 March 1974
Notes: Above date denotes when award was authorized for wear by U.S. Armed Forces personnel
Devices:

Republic of Vietnam Civil Actions Unit Citation

Instituted: 1966
Criteria: Awarded to certain units of the U.S. Armed Forces for meritorious service during the Vietnam War, 1 March 1961 to 28 March 1974
Devices:

Republic of Vietnam Campaign Medal

Instituted: 1966
Criteria: 6 months service in the Republic of Vietnam between 1961 and 1973 or if wounded, captured or killed in action during the above period
Devices:

★ The Military Ribbons of the Republic of Vietnam

Starting in the upper left-hand corner are military Decorations and Service Medals of the Republic of Vietnam. The awards are listed in the column to the right.

National Order of Vietnam, Commander (3rd class)
National Order of Vietnam, Knight or 5th class
Military Merit Medal
Army Distinguished Service Order 1st class
Army Distinguished Service Order 2d class
Air Force Distinguished Service Order
Navy Distinguished Service Order
Army Meritorious Service Medal
Air Force Meritorious Service Medal
Navy Meritorious Service Medal
Gallantry Cross with bronze star
Air Force Gallantry Cross
Navy Gallantry Cross
Special Service Medal
Hazardous Service Medal
Lifesaving Medal
Loyalty Medal
Wound Medal
Armed Honor Medal 1st class
Armed Honor Medal 2nd class
Leadership Medal
Staff service Medal 1st class and 2nd class
Technical Service Medal 1st class and 2nd class
Training Service Medal 1st class and 2nd class
Civic Actions Medal 1st class
Civic Action Medal 2nd class
Good Conduct Medal
Campaign Medal
Military Service Medal
Air Service Medal
Navy Service Medal, Unity Medal, Medal of Sacrifice

Medals of America Press 49

Foreign Decorations and Non-U.S. Service Awards

Philippine Defense Medal

Instituted: 1945

Criteria: Service in defense of the Philippines between 8 December 1941 and 15 June 1942

Devices: ★

Philippine Liberation Medal

Instituted: 1944

Criteria: Service in the liberation of the Philippines between 17 October 1944 and 3 September 1945

Devices: ★

Philippine Independence Medal

Instituted: 1946 (Army: 1948)

Criteria: Receipt of both the Philippine Defense and Liberation Medals/Ribbons. Originally presented to those present for duty in the Philippines on 4 July 1946

Devices: None

United Nations Service Medal (Korea)

Instituted: 1951

Criteria: Service on behalf of the United Nations in Korea between 27 June 1950 and 27 July 1954

Devices: None

Notes: Above date denotes when award was authorized for wear by U.S. military personnel.

United Nations Medal

Instituted: 1964

Criteria: 6 months service with any authorized U.N. operation:

Devices: ★

Notes: Above date denotes when award was authorized for wear by U.S. military personnel

Republic of Korea War Service Medal

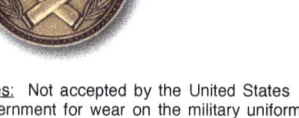

Instituted: 1951; approved for U. S. Veterans in 1999

Criteria: Service in Korean War theater for 30 consecutive days, or 60 nonconsecutive days

Devices: None*

Notes: Not accepted by the United States Government for wear on the military uniform until 1999.

* Some original 1953 medals had a taeguk in the center of the drape like the ribbon bar.

Marine Commemorative Medals for the Vietnam War

After the fall of the Republic and years passed, commemorative medals for veterans begin to appear in honor of significant events during the fighting. Not surprisingly, the first was a commemorative medal in honor of the Vietnamese Cross of Gallantry Unit Citation.

A very unique commemorative medal honors those who fought during Tet and saw their victory turned to a defeat by the media. The U.S. made Commeoratives shown all are manufactured to same quality and specifications as official American military medals.

Combat Action Commemorative Medal

Qualifying Dates: 1941-TBD

Criteria: Struck to honor all, marines who served in Comat Action

Navy Marine Presidential Unit Citation Commemorative Medal

Qualifying Dates: 1941-TBD

Criteria: Struck to honor all, sailors and marines who have been award the Presidential Unit Citation..

Navy Marine Unit Commemorative Medal

Criteria: Honors all Sailors and Marines awarded the Navy and Marine Unit Commendation Ribbon.

USMC Service Commemorative Medal

Instituted: 1939

Qualifying Dates: 1939 - Present

Criteria: Struck to honor all who honorably served in the USMC between 1939 and the present.

RVN Gallantry Cross Unit Citation Commemorative Medal

Qualifying Dates: 1965-1973

Criteria: Struck to honor all soldiers, sailors, marines and airmen who were awarded the RVN Gallantry Cross Unit Citation.

RVN Civil Action Unit Citation Commemorative Medal

Qualifying Dates: 1965-1973

Criteria: Struck to honor all soldiers, sailors, marines and airmen who were awarded the RVN Civil Action Honor Unit Citation.

Medals of America Press

Issue of U.S. Medals to Veterans, Retirees and Their Families

The Marine Corps normally issues decorations and service medals as they are awarded or earned. None of the U.S. Armed Services issue or replace any foreign awards, only United States awards.

Veterans of any United States military service may request medals never issued or replacement of medals which have been lost, stolen, destroyed or rendered unfit through no fault of their own. Requests may also be filed for awards that were earned but, for any reason, were never issued to the service member. A good example of this type of medal is the Korea Defense Service Medal which was approved in 2003 and back dated to cover everyone who served in Korea after 1954. More than 2 million former service personnel are now authorized this medal. The next-of-kin of deceased veterans may also make the same request for the medals of their veteran family member.

The National Personnel Records Center, Military Personnel Records (NPRC-MPR) is the repository of millions of military personnel, health, and medical records of discharged and deceased veterans of all services during the 20th and 21st century. Information from the records is made available upon written request (with signature and date) to the extent allowed by law.

There are two ways for those seeking information regarding military personnel records stored at NPRC (MPR). If you are a veteran or next-of-kin of a deceased veteran, you may now use vetrecs.archives.gov to order a copy of your military records. For all others, your request is best made using a Standard Form 180. It includes complete instructions for preparing and submitting requests.

Military Awards and Decorations

When you request issuance or replacement of military service medals, decorations, and awards, the National Personnel Records Center will verify the awards and forward the request with the verification to the appropriate Navy Personnel Command department for issuance of the medals.

The Standard Form (SF 180), Request Pertaining to Military Records, is recommended for requesting medals and awards. Provide as much information as possible and send the form to the appropriate address shown on the next page.

1. How to Obtain Standard Form 180 (SF-180), Request Pertaining to Military Records

   There are several ways to obtain an SF-180. You can:

   A. Download and print a copy of the SF-180 in PDF format by going to: http://www.archives.gov/facilities/mo/st_louis/military_personnel_records standard_form_180.html#sf.

   B. Order the form to be faxed to you from the National Archives and Records Administration's Fax-on-Demand System

      • Call the Fax-on-Demand System at (301) 837-0990 from a fax machine, using the handset.
      • Follow the voice instructions and request document number 2255.
      • There is no charge for this service except for any long distance telephone charges you may incur.

   C. Write to : National Personnel Records Center

      9700 Page Avenue, St. Louis, Missouri 63132.

   The SF 180 may be photocopied as needed but you must submit a separate SF 180 for each individual whose records are being requested.

2. Write a Letter to Request Medals. If you are not able to obtain SF-180, you may still submit a request for military medals by letter. The letter should indicate if the request is for a specific medal(s), or for all medals earned. It is also helpful to include copies of any military service documents that indicate eligibility for medals, such as military orders or the veteran's report of separation (DD Form 214 or its earlier equivalent).

Federal law [5 USC 552a(b)] requires that all requests for information from official military personnel files be submitted in writing. Each request must be signed (in cursive) by the veteran or his next-of-kin indicating the relationship to the deceased and dated (within the last year). For this reason, no requests are accepted over the internet.

Requests must contain enough information to identify the record among the more than 70 million on file at NPRC (MPR). Certain basic information is needed to locate military service records. This information includes:

- The veteran's complete name used while in service
- Service number or social security number
- Branch of service
- Dates of service
- Date and place of birth may also be helpful, especially if the service number is not known

If the request pertains to a record that may have been involved in the 1973 fire, also include:

- Place of discharge
- Last unit of assignment
- Place of entry into the service, if known

Please submit a separate request (either SF 180 or letter) for each individual whose records are being requested. Response times for records requested from the National Personnel Records Center (NPRC) vary greatly depending on the nature of the request. For example, the NPRC Military Records Facility currently has a backlog of 180,000 requests and receives approximately 5,000 requests per day. The center may have a difficult time locating records since millions of records were lost in a fire at the National Personnel Records Center in 1973. The fire destroyed 80 percent of the Army's discharge records between November 1912 and December 1959. World War II Army Air Force records were in this group. Seventy-five percent of the discharge records before 1964 and whose last names that fall alphabetically between Hubbard (James E.) and Z were also burned. Only four million records from this period were saved. Although the requested medals can often be issued on the basis of alternate records, the documents sent in with the request are sometimes the only means of determining proper eligibility.

Finally, you should exercise extreme patience. It may take several months or, in some cases, a year to determine eligibility and dispatch the appropriate medals. The center asks that you not send a follow-up request for 90 days. Because of these delays, many veterans simply purchase their medals from a supplier such as Medals of America.

Generally, there is no charge from the Marine Corps for medal or award replacements. The length of time to receive a response or your medals and awards varies depending upon the work load.

The Marine Corps processes requests for medals through the National Personnel Records Center, which determines eligibility through the information in the veteran's records. Once verified, a notification of entitlement is forwarded to Navy Personnel Command in Millington, Tennessee from which the medals are mailed to the requester.

To request medals earned while in the Marine Corps or by their next-of-kin write to:

National Personnel Records Center
1 Archives Drive
St. Louis, MO 63138

In case of a problem or an appeal write to:

Commandant of the Marine Corps
Military Awards Branch (MMMA)
2008 Elliot Road
Quantico, VA 22134

Cold War Recognition Certificate

In accordance with section 1084 of the Fiscal Year 1998 National Defense Authorization Act, the Secretary of Defense approved awarding Cold War Recognition Certificates to all members of the armed forces and qualified federal government civilian personnel who faithfully served the United States during the Cold War era, from Sept. 2, 1945 to Dec. 26, 1991. A quick search on the internet for Cold War certificate will provide the latest process for obtaining one.

A Cold War medal has been approved but the Department of Defense has no plans to strike one.

Veterans have the option of purchasing an unofficial Cold War Commemorative Medal for their service during the Cold War.

Cold War Recognition Certificate

Cold War Victory
Commemorative Medal

★ Vietnam Campaign Medals & DD214 Example

Good Conduct Medal • National Defense Service Medal • U.S. Vietnam Service Medal • Vietnam Campaign Medal • RVN Gallantry Cross Unit Citation

26. DECORATIONS, MEDALS, BADGES, COMMENDATIONS, CITATIONS AND CAMPAIGN RIBBONS AWARDED OR AUTHORIZED

Navy Achievement Medal w/"V", Combat Action Ribbon, Presidential Unit Citation w/2*, Meritorious Unit Commendation, Good Conduct Medal w/5*, National Defense Service Medal, Vietnam Service Medal w/5*, Republic of Vietnam Cross of Gallantry w/Bronze Star,

27. REMARKS

Item #26 continued: Republic of Vietnam Meritorious Unit Commendation w/palm & frame, Republic of Vietnam Meritorious Unit Commendation Civic Action Color 1st Class w/palm & frame, Republic of Vietnam Campaign Medal w/device, Rifle Expert Badge 3rd Award, Pistol Sharpshooter Badge, Letter of Commendation 1973, Certificate of Appreciation 1973, Letters of Appreciation 1973, 1974, 1975 (3). Served in Vietnam: 27 Oct 67 - 2 Nov 68. Extension of service was at the request and for the convenience of the Government.

This career Marine's discharge spells out his awards and uses the *symbol to indicate campaign and additional awards stars. Note the RVN Cross of Gallantry is listed w/bronze Star which means it is a personal decoration from the South Vietnamese government and not a unit award.

The Vietnam Service Medal with 5* will be represented by a single silver star (in lieu of 5 bronze stars) on the medal drape. The Combat Action Ribbon is the Navy/Marine Corps general equivalant of the Army Combat Infantry Badge.

Acronyms and Abbreviations:

AS	Air Medal -Strike /Flight	MOH	Medal of Honor
AH	Air Medal with "V" device	MSM	Meritorious Service Medal
AOE	Area of Eligibility	MUC	Meritorious Unit Commendation
BSM	Bronze Star Medal	NAM	Navy and Marine Corps Achievement Medal
BV	Bronze Star Medal with "V" device	NC	Navy and Marine Corps Commendation Medal
CAR	Combat Action Ribbon	NDSM	National Defense Service Medal
CE&S	Campaign, Expeditionary, and Service	NM	Navy and Marine Corps Medal
CMC	Commandant of the Marine Corps	NROTC	Naval Reserve Officer Training Corps
CNO	Chief of Naval Operations	NUC	Navy Unit Commendation
CO	Commanding Officer	NX	Navy Cross
CV	Navy and Marine Corps Commendation Medal with "V" device	PH	Purple Heart
		VCM	Republic of Vietnam Campaign Medal
		VSM	Vietnam Service Medal
DFC	Distinguished Flying Cross	PMD	Personal Military Decoration
DoD	Department of Defense	PNOK	Primary Next of Kin
DON	Department of the Navy	POWM	Prisoner of War Medal
DSM	Distinguished Service Medal	PTSD	Post Traumatic Stress Disorder
EH	Extraordinary Heroism	PUC	Presidential Unit Citation
EOT	End of Tour	RB	RVN Civil Action Medal
FMCR	Fleet Marine Corps Reserve	RC	RVN Civil Action Unit Award
FMF	Fleet Marine Force	RG	RVN Gallantry Cross Unit Award
FR	Fleet Reserve	RH	RVN Gallantry Cross Medal
HFP	Hostile Fire Pay	SECDEF	Secretary of Defense
MCGCM	Marine Corps Good Conduct Medal	SECNAV	Secretary of the Navy
LOM	Legion of Merit	SS	Silver Star Medal

54 Marine Corps Medals, Badges & Insignia Vietnam

★ Basic Vietnam Military Awards

After six months in country all Marines were authorized the Nadtional Defense Service Medal, the Vietnam Service Medal with campaign stars, the South Vietnam Campaign Medal and the RVN Gallantry Cross Unit Citiation and may have qualified for other awards.

Depending on his lenght of service an enlisted Marine could also have earned the USMC Good Conduct Medal along with the RVN Gallantry Cross Unit Citiation.

Medals of America Press 55

U.S. Marine Corps Vietnam Veterans' Awards Displays

Vietnam Service

500,000 Marines served in Vietnam from 1962 to 1975. From the DMZ and Khe Sanh to the battle of Hue and Dong Ha the largest field Marine Command ever employed. Shown here are examples of Marine Corps Vietnam Veterans' personal awards display cases.

Vietnam Service

Collar and Cover Insignia are displayed above the Purple Heart Medal, Navy Commedation and Achievement, Good Conduct, National Defense Service, Armed Forces Expeditionary Medal, Vietnam Service, RVN Gallantry Cross and RVN Campaign Medals. The Combat Action Ribbon and Navy PUC are shown above a name plate and Marksmanship Badges.

56 Marine Corps Medals, Badges & Insignia Vietnam

Vietnam Service

Collar and Cap Insignia are displayed above Navy Commedation, Good Conduct, National Defense Service, Vietnam Service, RVN Civil Actions, RVN Campaign Medals and 2 Commemorative Medals. The Combat Action Ribbon and Navy PUC are shown above a name plate and Marksmanship Badges. Other examples show mounted for wear medals in a display and the use of name plates to identify medals.

Medals of America Press 57

Other Great Medals and Insignia Books All Available at WWW.MOAPress.com or on Amazon

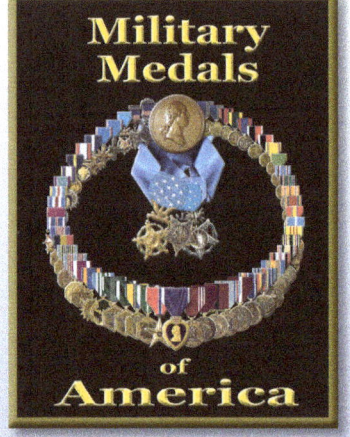
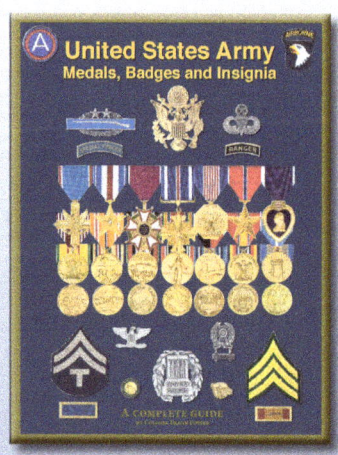

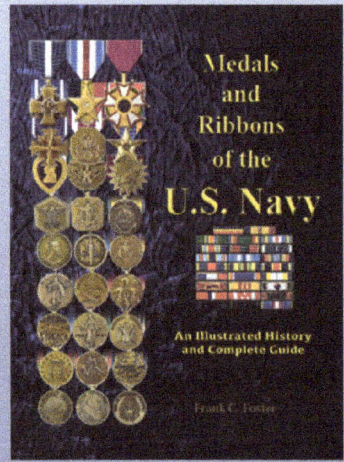
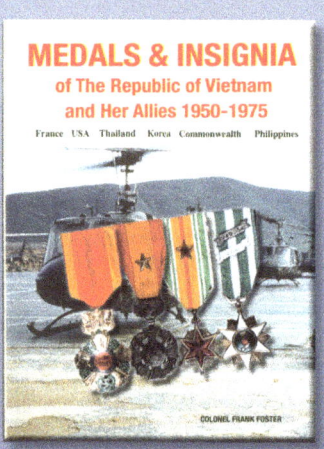
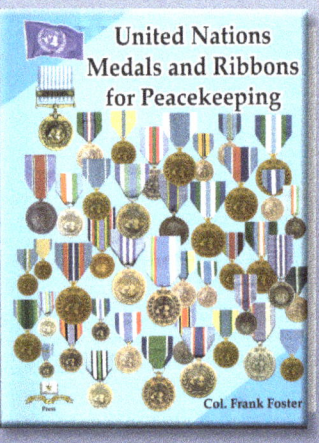
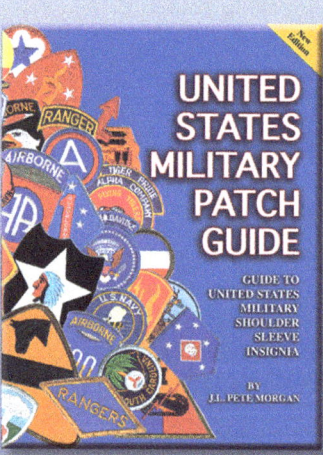

America's Best Medal and Ribbon Wear Guides All Available at WWW.MOAPress.com or on Amazon

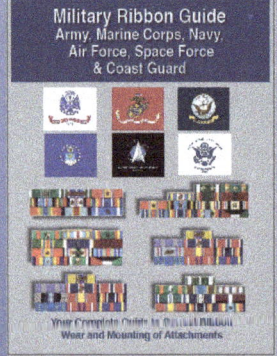

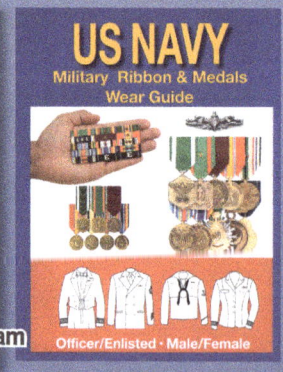

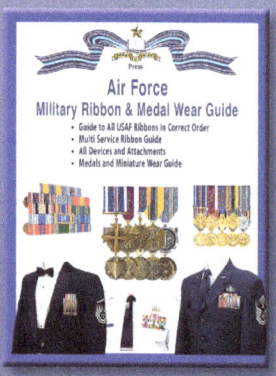

www.ingramcontent.com/pod-product-compliance
Lightning Source LLC
Chambersburg PA
CBHW051319110526
44590CB00031B/4409